Great World Writers

TWENTIETH CENTURY

EDITOR
PATRICK M. O'NEIL

Volume 2

Italo Calvino • Albert Camus • Alejo Carpentier

Aimé Césaire • Chou Shu-jen • J. M. Coetzee

Joseph Conrad • Tsitsi Dangarembga • Anita Desai

MARSHALL CAVENDISH
NEW YORK • TORONTO • LONDON • SYDNEY

Marshall Cavendish
99 White Plains Road
Tarrytown, New York 10591-9001

Website: www.marshallcavendish.com

Project Editor: Marian Armstrong
Development Editor: Thomas McCarthy
Editorial Director: Paul Bernabeo
Production Manager: Michael Esposito

Designer: Patrice Sheridan

Photo Research: Anne Burns Images
                            Carousel Research, Inc.
                                  Laurie Platt Winfrey
                                  Elizabeth Meryman
                                  Van Bucher
                                  Cristian Peña

Indexing: AEIOU
                 Cynthia Crippen

Library of Congress Cataloging-in-Publication Data

(Great world writers : twentieth century / editor, Patrick M. O'Neil.
      p. cm.
      Vol. 13 is an index volume.
      Includes bibliographical references and index.
      ISBN 0-7614-7469-2 (v. 1)—ISBN 0-7614-7470-6 (v. 2)—
ISBN 0-7614-7471-4 (v. 3)—ISBN 0-7614-7472-2 (v. 4)—
ISBN 0-7614-7473-0 (v. 5)—ISBN 0-7614-7474-9
(v. 6)—ISBN 0-7614-7475-7 (v. 7)—ISBN 0-7614-7476-5
(v. 8)—ISBN 0-7614-7477-3 (v. 9)—ISBN 0-7614-7478-1
(v. 10)—ISBN 0-7614-7479-X (v. 11)—ISBN 0-7614-7480-3
(v. 12)—ISBN 0-7614-7481-1 (v. 13 —ISBN 0-7614-7468-4 (set)
      1. Literature—20th century—Bio-bibliography—Dictionaries.
      2. Authors—20th century—Biography—Dictionaries.
      3. Literature—20th century—History and criticism. I.
      O'Neil, Patrick M.

PN771.G73 2004
809'.04—dc21
[B]   2003040922

Printed in China

09 08 07 06 05 04   6 5 4 3 2 1

Volume 2 Illustration Credits

Contents

Italo Calvino

BORN: October 15, 1923, Santiago de las Vegas, near Havana, Cuba
DIED: September 19, 1985, Siena, Italy
IDENTIFICATION: Italian novelist, journalist, essayist, and short-story writer whose humorous, fantastic, and experimental tales make him one of the twentieth century's most important and popular writers.

SIGNIFICANCE: A masterful and innovative storyteller, Italo Calvino is celebrated for his unique ability to combine reality with fantasy. The world is revealed to the reader through the eyes of his many "eyewitnesses"—antiheroic and nomadic characters whose wanderings wittily comment on war, poverty, commercialism, and technological progress. Calvino's writings span nearly four decades. His novels, short stories, and critical essays have been largely translated and are widely read and taught in schools and colleges all over the world.

The Writer's Life

Italo Calvino was born on October 15, 1923, in Santiago de las Vegas, a suburb of Havana, Cuba. Sentimentally named for his Italian heritage, he was the first of two sons of Italian parents, Mario and Evelina Mameli Calvino.

In 1925 the family returned to Italy to San Remo, a seaside town on the Italian Riviera, where Calvino's father ran an experimental floricultural center. Calvino's parents were botanists and agronomists and helped foster his keen interest in the natural sciences.

Childhood. Calvino grew up in the hills of beautiful San Remo in the midst of nature. He described his upbringing as generally happy, although his family life was a bit repressive. Throughout his childhood Calvino was an aspiring writer; his earliest goal was to write for the theater.

College and War Years. Partly to please his parents, in 1941 he enrolled at the University of Turin to study agriculture. After moving to the University of Florence, his studies were interrupted in 1943 by World War II, when he was called to serve in Mussolini's army. Rather than fight for the Fascists, Calvino went into hiding with his brother, Floriano; the pair then joined the partisan resistance, actively fighting against the Fascists and Nazis for 20 months.

After the war he returned to the University of Florence, where he changed his specialization to letters, graduating in 1947 with a thesis on the British author Joseph Conrad.

Initial Writings. After obtaining his degree, Calvino lived meagerly in Turin and focused his attention on refining his writing skills. In 1946 Calvino began working for the Turin publishing house Einaudi, a fruitful relationship that would be maintained until 1984. Calvino published his first novel, *Il sentiero dei nidi di ragno* (*The Path to the Spiders' Nest*), in 1947 to minor critical acclaim; it soon sold 6,000 copies and brought Calvino the prestigious Riccione prize.

An undated photograph of San Remo, Italy, and the surrounding hillside that formed Calvino's backyard growing up and fueled his deep interest in nature.

This group of young Italian men and women partisans of Pistoia, a province of Tuscany in western Italy, fought against Nazism by helping to ferret out German snipers and pockets of resistance in 1944, the same year Calvino and his brother, Floriano, joined the partisan resistance.

Politics. Calvino was influenced by his parents' antifascist political stance. After the war Calvino became a member of the Communist Party and worked for the party paper, *L'Unità,* where he published some of his first stories and began to be noticed in literary circles. In 1951 he traveled to Soviet Russia and finally left the Communist Party in 1957 as a result of the Soviet takeover of Hungary. He subsequently disavowed organized politics.

Writing Successes in Italy and Abroad.
With the publication of *Fiabe italiane* (*Italian Folktales*) in 1956, Calvino received international recognition. From then on he was widely

translated, and works such as *Le cosmicomiche* (*Cosmicomics,* 1965), *Le città invisibili* (*Invisible Cities,* 1972), and *Se una notte d'inverno un viaggiatore* (*If on a Winter's Night a Traveler,* 1979) were read worldwide. Within his own country he received multiple awards for his work, including the Bagutta, Feltrinelli, and Asti Prizes.

Calvino's literary activity continued to critical acclaim until his death. In addition to his numerous novels and collections of short stories, he founded, with the Italian novelist Elio Vittorini, the notable journal *Menabò* and wrote opera librettos and newspaper articles and was engaged with the experimental French literary circles Tel Quel and Oulipo.

Last Years.

After returning to Rome in 1980, Calvino spent much of the last five years of his life writing and traveling. In 1981 he received the prestigious Italian Legion of Honor and officiated at the Venice film festival. In 1983 he traveled to New York and Paris to give lectures and in 1984 ventured to Argentina and subsequently to Seville, Spain, where he was invited, with the Argentinean writer Jorge Luis Borges, to a conference on fantastic literature. In the same year he also ended his 38-year relationship with Einaudi and accepted an offer from Garzanti, a Milanese publishing house.

Calvino spent part of the last year of his life preparing *Lezioni americane: Sei proposte per il prossimo millennio (Six Memos for the Next Millennium),* a sequence of conferences that he was to deliver as part of the prestigious Norton Lecture Series at Harvard University. He finished only five of the six lectures; he had a stroke on September 6 at Castiglione della Pescaia, a seaside town in Tuscany, and died in the hospital in Siena as a result of a cerebral hemorrhage on September 19. Calvino is buried in the hilltop cemetery in Castiglione della Pescaia. Calvino's successes continued after his death, as his wife and daughter posthumously published many of his works.

Calvino relaxing in France in 1981, the same year he was awarded the esteemed Italian Legion of Honor.

Travels and Family.

Calvino had a love for travel and adventure; in 1959 and 1960 he spent six months in the United States, mostly in New York, a city he greatly loved. He journeyed to Paris, where in 1962 he met Esther Judith Singer (called Chichita), an Argentinean translator. The couple married in Havana, Cuba, in 1964, and in 1965 their only child, Giovanna, was born in Rome. In 1967 the family moved to Paris where they would live for 13 years. While in Paris, Calvino continued his travels to America, Mexico, and Japan, returning to Italy most summers.

Calvino wrote novels, short stories, opera librettos, fairytales, and nonfiction. He is best known for his short fiction; many of his novels are essentially collections of shorter tales. Calvino had a love for storytelling; his tales are often humorous, chronicling the adventures of his likable protagonists.

Issues in Calvino's Fiction. Calvino dealt with many subjects, and his writings belong to several genres. He wrote war stories, fairytales, science fiction, fantasy novels, and experimental tales. His numerous themes include World War II, lost childhood innocence, the urban experience, impossible love, and travels in time and space. In his fiction he blends science with fantasy and realism with imagination and reinvents historical data.

Calvino's writings often reflect social, economic, and political issues in contemporary Italy and include topics such as the effects of World War II and the disillusionment of the so-called economic boom of the 1950s and 1960s. He also wrote novels that were extremely experimental and self-referential. As varied as it was, his fiction was extremely popular with many age groups.

People in Calvino's Fiction. Calvino's most typical protagonists are witty and agreeable male antiheroes. They are often onlookers, watching and then commenting on the many adventures that they witness. Several of Calvino's characters doubt not only their own makeup but also that of the people and places surrounding them. This interest in the instability of the self and one's environment reflects Calvino's attraction to what is uncertain and unknown rather than what is clear and accepted.

Among Calvino's most outstanding characters are the child protagonist and resistance fighter Pin, from *The Path to the Spiders' Nest*, and Marcovaldo, the childlike father who searches out nature in the industrial city, in *Marcovaldo, ovvero le stagioni in città,* (*Marcovaldo, or the*

Seasons in the City, 1963). These characters share a type of naive innocence unsuited to their social worlds. Precisely within this paradox may be found what fascinated the author the most: the realm of the unknown.

The Theme of Adventure. Most of Calvino's fiction deals with adventures in love, travel, reading, and other amusements. Some escapades are quite ordinary in scope, such as two people sitting next to each other on a train in "L'avventura di un soldato" ("The Adventure of a Soldier," 1958) or a trip to the grocery store ("Marcovaldo al supermarket"), while others, such as *Il barone*

A Night in Bologna, 1958, Paul Cadmus's egg tempera-on-fiberboard artwork, illuminates two of Calvino's more prominent themes: war and unrequited love.

rampante (*The Baron in the Trees*, 1957), take on such considerable issues as the disappearing aristocracy, utopia, and the French Revolution. There is no finality or straightforward conclusion to these adventures, as both the protagonists and the reader are left with more questions than answers.

BIBLIOGRAPHY

Adler, Sara. *Calvino, the Writer as Fablemaker.* Potomac, MD: Porrúa Turanzas, 1979.

Jeannet, Angela. *Under the Radiant Sun and the Crescent Moon: Italo Calvino's Storytelling.* Toronto: University of Toronto Press, 2000.

Markey, Constance. *Italo Calvino: A Journey toward Postmodernism.* Gainesville: University Press of Florida, 1999.

McLaughlin, Martin. *Italo Calvino.* Edinburgh, UK: Edinburgh University Press, 1998.

Re, Lucia. "Calvino and the Value of Literature." *MLN* 113, no. 1 (1998).

Ricci, Franco, ed. *Calvino Revisited.* Ottawa: Dovehouse, 1989.

Weiss, Beno. *Understanding Italo Calvino.* Columbia: University of South Carolina Press. 1993.

HIGHLIGHTS IN CALVINO'S LIFE

1923	Italo Calvino is born on October 15 in Santiago de las Vegas, near Havana, Cuba.
1925	Returns home with his family to San Remo, Italy.
1941	Studies agriculture at the University of Turin.
1943	Transfers to the University of Florence; is called to fight for Mussolini's Fascist government but goes into hiding for some months.
1944	With his brother, Floriano, joins the partisan resistance.
1945	Returns to the University of Florence, switching his specialization to literature; is active in the Communist Party.
1946	Begins work with the Einaudi publishing house.
1947	Earns his degree and publishes his first novel, *The Path to the Spiders' Nest.*
1955	Becomes the director at Einaudi.
1957	Leaves the Communist Party.
1962	Meets Esther Judith Singer, his future wife.
1964	Marries Esther in Havana.
1965	Daughter, Giovanna, is born; Calvino publishes *Cosmicomics.*
1967–1968	Moves to Paris and frequents the city's literary circles.
1972	Wins the Feltrinelli Prize for literature; publishes *Invisible Cities.*
1980	Moves back to Rome.
1981	Is awarded the Italian Legion of Honor.
1983	Publishes *Palomar.*
1985	Dies in Siena on September 19.

COSMICOMICS

Genre: Short stories
Subgenre: Fantasy
Published: Turin, 1965
Time period: The future
Setting: Travels in time and space

Themes and Issues. The title of Calvino's collection is revealing of its themes. He blends the "cosmos" (science) with "comics" (humor and the imagination). The tales of *Cosmicomics* deal with substantial scientific issues, including the formation of the universe, the speed of light, and human evolution. The dazzling stories demystify scientific beliefs, as hypothesis is combined with fantasy and romance in order to posit alternative evolutionary possibilities.

The Plot. Qfwfq, *Cosmicomics'* time-and-space-traveling and shape-shifting narrator, depicts fantastic and magical worlds. Each of the 12 stories begins with a brief scientific description of cosmic phenomenon that Qfwfq, who has existed as lifeforms such as mollusks and dinosaurs, recounts.

The first story, "The Distance of the Moon," treats the moon's rotation around Earth and is an excellent example of Calvino's ability to combine science with the emotions. In Calvino's version the moon comes so close to Earth that it is possible to climb up on it, and that is exactly what Qfwfq and his friends do. Every month they go searching for moon milk; during one cycle the moon pulls away too quickly, and Qfwfq's deaf cousin, who is enamored of the moon, and Mrs. Vhd, who is in love with Qfwfq's cousin, are trapped on the lunar surface.

"At Daybreak" addresses the materialization of the first rays of sunlight and their effects on a previously motionless and formless family. "All at One Point" deals with the theory of the big bang, racism, and adolescent sexuality.

Human evolution is combined with unrequited love in "Without Colors," "The Dinosaurs," and "The Spiral." Betting, rivalry, and competition as the cosmos develops are the main focuses of "A Sign in Space" and "The Light-Years."

Analysis. The light, imaginative, and evocative tone of *Cosmicomics* ironically critiques the industrialization of contemporary society. Although Qfwfq makes several references to modern technologies, including train stations and Swiss banks, the narrative's emphasis is on the imagination and the fantastic.

Heriberto Mora's oil painting *The Instrument* can be imaginatively transformed, as Calvino would combine hypothesis with fantasy, to create the perfect lunar playground and source of fascination for the characters in "The Distance of the Moon," the first story in Calvino's 1965 collection of short stories, *Cosmicomics.*

In all of Qfwfq's amorous journeys, authentic emotional sentiment is rarely reciprocated. Although love and desire are what create and expand the universe, more often than not Qfwfq loses his loved one and feels lonely or nostalgic for what he never possessed. Through these unfulfilled relationships, Calvino reflects upon absolute origin and identity, as well as difference and multiplicity.

SOURCES FOR FURTHER STUDY

Cannon, JoAnn. *Italo Calvino: Writer and Critic.* Ravenna: Longo, 1981.

Vlasopolos, Anca. "Love and the Two Discourses in *Le cosmicomiche.*" *Stanford Italian Review* 4, no. 1 (1984).

PALOMAR

Genre: Novel
Subgenre: Memoir
Published: Turin, 1983
Time period: Early 1980s
Setting: Italy, France, Spain, Japan, Mexico

Themes and Issues. In this, Calvino's last novel, as in *Marcovaldo* and *La giornata d' uno scrutatore* (*The Watcher,* 1963), the title character appraises all that surrounds him. Mr. Palomar's name deliberately evokes the famous telescope near San Diego; he is a passionate observer, continuously probing into the intricacies of his world.

Next to the index of the novel, the author explains the three main experiences to be derived from his tales: visual, cultural, and speculative, all sharing the idea of perception and the desire—at times unfulfilled—for comprehension.

This novel deals with two other themes central to Calvino's writing. The isolation of the individual in contemporary society is a theme evident in the melancholy "The Albino Gorilla," in which Mr. Palomar compares himself to the uprooted and isolated ape Snowflake. The second theme, concerning the limits of knowledge and difficulties of choice, is apparent in "The Cheese Museum"; in this story Mr. Palomar cannot decide which cheeses to buy, and his indecision nearly costs him his place in a lengthy line.

SOME INSPIRATIONS BEHIND CALVINO'S WORK

His texts are colored by having lived next to the ocean, both in his youth and later in his life. *Palomar* and many of his short stories take place at the seaside.

At age 12 Calvino was profoundly influenced by Rudyard Kipling's *The Jungle Book;* he became an avid reader, continually searching out the same pleasure in other books that he found in Kipling's tales. As a boy, Calvino was fascinated by comic strips and loved spending time at the movies, where he viewed innumerable films; these solitary experiences influenced his future writing.

Finally, Calvino's experiences in the war inspired his first novel and some collections of short stories, including *Ultimo viene il corvo* (*The Crow Comes Last,* 1949).

John Winship's 2000 work of art *Seated Man (Oceanside)* reflects Calvino's lifetime love of the ocean and his desire for constant introspection.

LONG FICTION

1947 Il sentiero dei nidi di ragno (The Path to the Spiders' Nest)
1963 Marcovaldo, ovvero le stagioni in città (Marcovaldo, or the Seasons in the City)
1963 La giornata d'uno scrutatore (The Watcher)
1965 Le cosmicomiche (Cosmicomics)
1972 Le città invisibili (Invisible Cities)
1979 Se una notte d'inverno un viaggiatore (If on a Winter's Night a Traveler)

1983 Palomar

COLLECTIONS OF STORIES

1949 Ultimo viene il corvo (The Crow Comes Last)
1954 L'entrata in guerra (Entering the War)
1956 Fiabe italiane (Italian Folktales)
1957 Il barone rampante (The Baron in the Trees)
1958 I racconti (Short Stories)
1991 Romanzi e Racconti (Novels and Short Stories)

ESSAYS AND OTHER WRITINGS

1988 Lezioni americane: Sei proposte per il prossimo millennio (Six Memos for the Next Millennium)
1991 Perchè leggere i classici (Why Read the Classics)
1995 Saggi, 1945-1985 (Essays, 1945-1985)

The Plot. The novel is divided into three sections: Mr. Palomar's vacations at the seaside, his experiences in the city, and his silences. Each of the 27 tales details Mr. Palomar's thoughts and reactions. Natural occurrences that he contemplates include the motion of waves, a ray of sunlight, the planets and stars, and the universe acting as mirror. He is acutely fascinated by humans and animals, pondering a topless sunbather, mating turtles, a gecko's stomach, and running giraffes. While in the city he is captivated by the goings-on at a butcher shop and at home by a pair of mismatched slippers.

Analysis. Although written in the third person, this amusing and graceful collection is clearly semiautobiographical, chronicling and reflecting on the last years of the author's life. The main protagonist is Calvino's age and, like Calvino, he prefers silence and reflection to the noise and commotion of contemporary society. Akin to Calvino, Mr. Palomar lives between Rome and the seaside and is an avid traveler.

The last tale in the collection, "Learning to be Dead," is exceptionally memorable and moving. Mr. Palomar is, as the title suggests, living his life as if he were dead, dying precisely when he decides to describe each moment from his life, mistakenly feeling that until he has done so, death can be avoided. The author's imminent passing makes this final deliberation even more poignant.

SOURCES FOR FURTHER STUDY

Biasin, Gian Paolo. "The Surface of Things, the Depth of Words." In *Calvino Revisited.* Ottawa: Dovehouse, 1989.
Lucente, Gregory L. "An Interview with Italo Calvino." *Contemporary Literature* 26, no. 3 (1985).

Other Works

INVISIBLE CITIES (1972). In *Invisible Cities,* an experimental collection, the Venetian traveler Marco Polo describes to the Tartar emperor Kublai Khan the many cities he encountered during his voyages. Calvino roughly based his dreamlike and abstract tales on Marco Polo's

Travels, which chronicle the explorer's journeys from Europe to Asia between 1271 and 1295.

In Calvino's rendition the pair sits in Khan's garden. Khan senses that the sun is setting on both his life and empire, and to entertain and distract Khan, Marco Polo intricately describes 55 cities that he has visited. The text is elaborately ordered, following a complex structure that reveals Calvino's interest in mathematics and science. Each of the nine chapters begins and

John Wilde's 1970 work of art *Wildeview* depicts an individual much like Mr. Palomar, the fervent observer who views the realistic and the obscure from an isolated vantage point, sometimes living his life as if he were already dead, in Calvino's semiautobiographical final novel, *Palomar.*

ends with a conversation between Kubla Khan and Marco Polo. In total, Marco Polo intuitively illustrates five cities from each of the 11 different categories: memory, desire, signs, eyes, names, the dead, the sky, thin cities, trading cities, continuous cities, and hidden cities.

As the title implies, the cities are invisible: each metropolis has magical, fantastic, and dreamlike qualities rather than concrete and realistic traits. There is little action or narrative development. Rather, the tales raise philosophical and moral questions regarding the nature of language, utopia and politics, the imaginary and the real, and death and life.

Resources

Major collections of Calvino manuscripts can be found in the libraries of the University of California at Los Angeles, Columbia University, and Yale University. Other points of reference to students of Calvino include the following:

Audio Special: Celebrating Italo Calvino. This is an audio file where many important writers discuss Calvino's work and read translations of his fiction (http://www.nytimes.com/books/99/10/31/specials/calvino.html).

Calvino on the Internet. Many complete texts of Calvino's can be found on-line in English. "Italo Calvino" (http://www.emory.edu/EDUCATION/mfp/cal.html) and "Outside the town of Malbork" (http://www.msu.edu/~comertod/calvino.htm) are two wonderful Web sites housing writings by and about Calvino.

DANA RENGA

Albert Camus

BORN: November 7, 1913, Mondovi, Algeria

DIED: January 4, 1960, Sens, France

IDENTIFICATION: French novelist, dramatist, and journalist whose work sympathetically examines the absurdity of existence and espouses the need for disinterested and humane action.

SIGNIFICANCE: Camus, a French Algerian from an impoverished family and a man with a history of tuberculosis, used his prodigious talent to help the human condition to be understood and ameliorated wherever possible. His writing is noted for energy, passion, and above all, sincerity and lack of pretense. At the time he received the Nobel Prize in 1957—he was one of the youngest to win this award—he had already written three worldwide classics. *The Stranger* (1942), *The Plague* (1947), and *The Fall* (1956) show entangled motives and inexplicable evil. His ironic death in a sports car accident served as the final metaphor of absurdity, merging his life with his art.

The Writer's Life

Some of the dilemmas inherent in Albert Camus's life and work come from the time and place of his birth in Algeria on November 7, 1913: His family belonged to the colonizing power in Algeria yet were low-level laborers. His membership in the overlord class collided with his undeniably humane perspective. Overtly sympathetic to his fellow poor yet intermittently oblivious to the native Arabs and Kabylas (a Berber group), he held simplistic views on causes and cures for Algeria. This paradoxical blind spot persists into his fiction and brought him into bitter controversies. Camus alienated each extreme with a plea for the middle way.

Early Life. Losing his father before he was a year old, Camus grew up under the guidance of a severe maternal grandmother and a doting but nearly mute and completely illiterate mother. In the cramped tenement room lived also his brother, four years older, and two maternal uncles. His mother worked as a cleaning woman and also had a widow's pension, indispensable sources of income that paid for his early schooling and medical care. A quick learner and a good soccer player, Camus, through competitive examinations, secured a lycée education as a scholarship student. His graduation from the lycée (roughly equivalent to a college preparatory curriculum plus junior

This group photograph includes Albert Camus as a child. Dressed in black and seated in the center, he poses at the studio of one of his uncles in Algiers in 1920.

college) was delayed by the onset of tuberculosis when he was 17. An uncle and aunt moved him into their more sanitary apartment to recover. Henceforth, he was on his own. With a scholarship to the university, he pursued a Diploma of Advanced Studies, roughly equivalent to a bachelor of arts degree with honors, with a thesis on Plotinus and Saint Augustine.

Camus married Simone Hié, a fellow student, on June 16, 1934. What was to be her lifelong drug addiction brought an end to the marriage in 1936, although Simone's mother, who was a physician, would ask Camus for moral support for the rest of his life. Because of his tubercular condition, Camus was declared unfit for a teaching position. In the meantime, as a leftist journalist, he joined the Communist Party, which ejected him in 1938 for not supporting the party line on Arab nationalism. His lifelong admiration of André Malraux began at this time. It would later lead him to support Malraux's political leader, Charles De Gaulle. When the *Alger Républicain* was shut down by the authorities, Camus went to work for *Le Soir Républicain*. When it in turn was shut down in January 1940, he left for Paris to work at *Paris-Soir*. When the German invasion began, the staff moved to Clermont-Ferrand. In December he married Francine Faure. In 1941 they returned to her home in Oran, Algeria, the setting for *The Plague*.

From 1941 until his death, Camus would alternate between a hectic pace and enforced rest. He combined a life of theater, journalism, and publishing with late nights and beautiful women. Until his wife's death in 1979, the larger world of readers and scholars supposed that he was like Dr. Rieux, the celibate, self-effacing physician who records the course of the

Francine Camus was the author's on-again, off-again wife and confidante. Plagued by mental instability, she became the inspiration for the drowning woman in her husband's 1956 novel, *The Fall,* in which an esteemed Paris lawyer fails to come to the woman's aid. Slim recompense for Camus's serial infidelity, she later told her husband, "You owed me that book," and the author agreed.

epidemic in *The Plague*. Camus was a Don Juan whose egoistic personal conscience coexisted with a selfless social conscience. Once Camus took a mistress, unlike Don Juan, he rarely dropped her; she remained in his life. Like Don Juan, Camus, regardless of his age, always chose new women in their early 20s.

In 1941, overextended, Camus wrote the play *Caligula,* and the essay "The Myth of Sisyphus" in tandem with *The Stranger.* The publication of the last in 1942 coincided with a severe relapse of tuberculosis, requiring the couple to go to a retreat in the Chambon area of France. (The Allies occupied Oran the same year.)

HIGHLIGHTS IN CAMUS'S LIFE

1913   Albert Camus is born in Mondovi, Algeria on November 7.

1914   Father dies October 14 in Battle of the Marne in World War I; his mother moves him and his brother to Algiers.

1930   Camus suffers first onslaught of tuberculosis.

1934   Marries Simone Hié on June 16, despite her drug addiction.

1935   Joins Communist Party; lifelong admiration of André Malraux begins.

1936   Camus receives Diploma of Advanced Studies; takes kayak trip from Innsbruck through Czechoslovakia (site of *The Misunderstanding*); separates from Simone.

1936–1937 Makes professional commitment to amateur theatricals; serves as secretary at Algiers Cultural Center.

1938   Leaves Communist Party; is declared medically unfit for teaching certificate.

1938   Joins editorial staff of *Alger Républicain,* devoted to Popular Front policies of Léon Blum.

1939   Starts working for another daily, *Le Soir Républicain.*

1940   *Le Soir Républicain* is shut down by authorities; Camus moves to Paris to work on *Paris-Soir;* moves with staff to Clermont-Ferrand when Hitler's invasion begins; marries Francine Faure; writes *Caligula,* "Myth of Sisyphus," and *The Stranger* in tandem.

1941   Returns with Francine to Oran.

1942   Publishes *The Stranger;* suffers severe tuberculosis relapse; moves with Francine to the Chambon in France for recuperation.

1943   Camus moves to Paris to work for Gallimard; joins *Combat,* a resistance publication.

1944   Paris is liberated on August 24.

1945   German surrender is announced May 8; widespread violent demonstrations break out in Algeria; Francine gives birth to twins; *Caligula* opens to great success on September 15.

1946   Camus visits the United States.

1947   Leaves *Combat;* publishes *The Plague,* which receives Critics Prize.

1951   Publishes *The Rebel.*

1953–1954 Depression requires wife's institutionalization.

1955   Distressed over state of emergency in Algeria, Camus contributes to *L'Express.*

1956   Publishes *The Fall.*

1957   Wins Nobel Prize on October 16.

1959   Produces an adaptation of Dostoyevsky's *The Possessed.*

1960   Dies in a sports car accident on January 4.

In 1943 Camus began work for Gallimard publishers in Paris and joined *Combat,* a resistance publication, where he stayed on until June 1947. In his personal life the liberation of Paris on August 24, 1943, also saw his initial liaison with the actress Maria Casarès, who broke with him when she learned that his wife was pregnant. The German surrender in May 1945 triggered widespread violent demonstrations in Algeria. In September Camus's wife gave birth to twins, Jean and Catherine, and *Caligula* began a successful run. From mid-March to May 1946, he made a tour of the Northeastern United States and began a liaison with Patricia Blake.

In 1947 Camus left Combat and published *The Plague,* which received the Critics Prize. Maria Casarès reentered his life in 1948 as his "official" mistress. In July and August 1949 he made a tour of Brazil, Chile, and Uruguay and began antibiotic treatment for his tuberculosis. In October 1951 he published *The Rebel,* which received widespread mixed reviews. A long, belittling review in *Les temps modernes,* the monthly published by the writer and philosopher Jean-Paul Sartre, led to acrimonious public controversy and a permanent rift with Marxists and existentialists, with whom he had long been linked. His womanizing, combined with his exasperation with domesticity and fatherhood, drove his wife to depression and institutionalization. (Francine recognized herself as the suicide in *The Fall.* After she broke her pelvis in a suicide attempt, her family asked him to stop living with her. Eventually she resumed her life as a mathematics teacher.) Camus became a contributor to *L'Express* in order to have a forum for his moderate midway course for Algeria, by then in a state of emergency. In January 1956 he appealed to a large crowd of Algiers moderates for a truce. In May he published *The Fall* and took the actress Catherine Sellers

as his latest mistress. In March he published a collection of short stories, *Exile and the Kingdom.* On October 15, 1957, while lunching with Patricia Blake in a Parisian restaurant, he learned he had won the Nobel Prize. His first words to the press were, "It should have gone to Malraux." He also said that since his wife had done the suffering, she had a right to the reward. He in a rented tuxedo and she in a borrowed ermine stole played man and wife for the Swedish press. In 1959 he produced *Les possédés,* an adaptation of Dostoyevsky's *The Possessed.* He was also working on *The First Man.* On January 4, 1960, he was killed instantly when the sports car in which he was riding hit a tree. As in one of his works, where every prop counts as a symbol, in the photograph of the accident, the automobile against the tree looks like a mechanical crucifixion.

Camus pauses outside his home in 1955. In his fictive world, exterior spaces are often collapsed and internalized.

The son of an early World War I casualty, Camus was reared in Algiers in dire poverty; he lived in slum conditions with his autocratic maternal grandmother and beloved mute mother. As teachers interceded to secure him lycée and university educations, he moved from an atmosphere of defiant illiteracy to classical erudition without losing his sense of fond home ties. By the age of 17, unsanitary living conditions and overwork had brought on tuberculosis, which interrupted his life from time to time thereafter but also strengthened his belief in the preciousness of life. These events, each and every one, left their mark on the writer that Camus was to become.

Issues in Camus's Work. Camus is a classical moralist in the French sense: his writing has a unified point of view, and he uses as few words as possible to convey his intent, with concise description that is never belabored and realistic dialogue. The end result has a strong moral thrust. The moral may be extraordinarily ambiguous (in the case of *The Stranger* it is to a significant extent a function of the translation one reads), but readers know that they are to identify and ponder the moral issues raised. In his works that employ first-person narration, it is clear that Camus himself is not the "I," but neither does he work to subvert the narrative consciousness. Readers are given total freedom to assess what they have read. This freedom to think through the fiction is probably the reason why readers may dislike some characters but still like the author.

Readers also have the option of supplying what Camus omits: the steady pressure of the Arabs and the Berber population of Algeria for independence from French rule. Indeed, to admire Camus may require factoring out his blind spot as he factors out the non-Western populations in everything he wrote about Algeria. Such a blindspot was likely a coping strategy for growing up in Algeria, as he did, where economically his family was no better off than the general Arab population. His work implies a recognition of unsolvable inequities: life is a back-and-forth, an eerie truce with aliens beneath and around him and the French upper classes above him.

At bottom, Camus works through social and ethical problems case by case and eschews sweeping decisions that sacrifice life for an unknowable utopian end. (Not surprisingly, his membership in the Communist Party was brief.) This position is seen clearly in Camus's statement at a stormy meeting with students in Sweden at the time of his Nobel award. His interpreter, Carl-Gustav Bjurström, has reconstructed Camus's reply: "Bombs are being thrown in the trolleys of Algiers, and my mother

Camus lent his voice to the restless and questing contemporary figure, striving for greater clarity and order. "You will never be happy if you continue to search for what happiness consists of," he warned. "You will never live if you are looking for the meaning of life."

Camus's moral outlook was deeply influenced by his many years in Algeria. "I believe in justice," he wrote, "but I will defend my mother before justice," referring to his native land in maternal terms. For Algeria to be truly free, he argued, it needed to be liberated not only from the French army, but also from domestic terrorism. "The cause of the Arab people of Algeria has never been worse served than by terrorism against civilians, now practiced systematically by Arab movements. Terrorism delays, perhaps irremediably, the solution of justice that will eventually come."

might find herself in one of those trolleys; if that's your justice, I prefer my mother to justice."

Commonsense Existentialism. Although Camus may be read from a postcolonial perspective, in his lifetime he was labeled an existentialist writer—a label both he and the existentialists rejected. His personal loyalties and less formidable philosophical education kept him out of their inner circles. In fact, a hostile review of his personally conceived social philosophy, *The Rebel* (1951), in the more or less official existentialist periodical *Les temps modernes* (May 1952) veritably excommunicated him from this particular Marxist elite. Still, what readers at midcentury found appealing in his work could be called a humanistic existentialism writ large. The human condition in the best of circumstances is riddled with accidents, disappointments, poverty, disease, and inevitably, death. It is absurd—absurd to struggle, absurd to stay alive. Yet human beings, as his spokesperson Dr. Rieux says in *The Plague,* manifest more to admire than deplore, and human failure and crime serve to make success and sainthood more clearly understood.

Characters bent upon achieving sainthood are perceptive observers and demonstrate lucidity—or else they acquire it in spite of themselves. Thus, while readers are always aware of being told a story, they can overhear restrained lyrical outbursts when the narrator is diverted by beauty or pleasure. The sense that such enjoyment comes on borrowed time adds to the poignancy of the lyrical intrusion.

Overt Metaphors. Camus depends on extended metaphors to imply a complex of possible meanings. That is, plot is itself a metaphor within the fiction and a metaphor for life generally. In his drama, which has had only limited success outside France, he preferred to adapt novels written in this metaphoric mode to the stage, but his few original dramas show this impulse also. The plots themselves, while open ended, also give a sense of completion, of fulfillment: an action is prepared for and carried out, and its consequences are reaped. Further, the ending conveys a sense of cosmic justice, popularly defined, and usually common decency as well.

To create characters who would be recognized

SOME INSPIRATIONS BEHIND CAMUS'S WORK

The influences on Camus's work were largely nonliterary, and there is in fact little precedent in French literature for the prose of *The Stranger,* at once so emotionally hard to pin down yet seemingly so simple and straightforward on the surface, at the level of the words themselves. Camus admitted to an affection for the terse, unadorned style of hard-boiled American detective novels, and some of their flavor survives in his work. To some extent the moral concerns of Saint Augustine, on whom he had written his thesis, never ceased to influence his outlook, and it is clear that the work of his friend André Malraux moved and inspired him deeply, especially Malraux's great novel *La condition humaine* (1933), which is widely known by its English title, *Man's Fate.* Above all else, he valued the sublimity of nature, especially Algeria, where life was a risky affair for the colonists. He was to die before Algerian independence, but the rhythm of repression and reprisal marked him—and everything—he wrote deeply.

Albert Camus (center), known for being an animated and energetic director, rehearses actors at a theater festival in Angers, in western France. Though hardly a successful dramatist, Camus never lost his love of the theater. "It is the only place where one can find innocent happiness," he said.

in daily life (and the prototypes did recognize themselves), to develop plots with self-propelling action, and to contrive overall metaphors of moral imperatives in relatively short novels, Camus was obliged not just to choose words carefully but also to exploit the multifaceted complexity of the French language. Any object or event mentioned has symbolic implications. For example, the food eaten by the narrator in *The Stranger*, the novel a volunteer medical aide is writing in *The Plague*, the painting the speaker of *The Fall* is hiding—all were conscious authorial choices to point readers to moral implications. Because so much meaning and emotive force rests with individual nouns and specific

verb tenses and modes, Camus's translators have had a considerable responsibility placed upon them. (The French syntax and grammar themselves are not difficult. Camus's works are often read in French language classes.)

BIBLIOGRAPHY

Judt, Tony. *The Burden of Responsibility: Blum, Camus, Aron.* Chicago: University of Chicago Press, 1998.

—. *Past Imperfect. French Intellectuals 1944–1956.* Berkeley: University of California Press, 1992.

Todd, Olivier. *Albert Camus: A Life.* Translated by Benjamin Ivry. New York: Knopf, 1997.

Vulor, Ena C. *Colonial and Anti-Colonial Discourses.* Lanham, MD: University Press of America, 2000.

Translating The Stranger

Provocative as it may sound, it would not be entirely wrong to say that for 43 years, third-year French students reading *L'étranger* were not reading the same novel as were their classmates reading Stuart Gilbert's 1945 translation, *The Stranger*. This state of affairs persisted until 1988, when Matthew Ward retranslated the novel. Though Gilbert's *Stranger* is still readable and, in a real sense, accurate, when a book has become a classic, retranslation is both necessary and inevitable.

Gilbert (1888–1969), like any translator, picked up some cues and missed or downplayed others. Scapegoating seems to have especially concerned him, and so he made lexical and grammatical choices that show a more humane Meursault playing a predetermined role in a social ritual. Ward (1951–1990) encountered *The Stranger* first through Gilbert's translation. Wanting, as he put it, to show the real Meursault, he decided to be quite literal: "I have . . . attempted to capture what he [Camus] said and how he said it, not what he meant."

A translator's problems begin with the title: *l'étranger* means "stranger," but it also means "foreigner," "outsider," and "alien." The next problem is the first sentence: the identity in form in French between "has died" and "is dead" gives the translator a choice between concern (Gilbert) and indifference (Ward).

The choices continue. For example, Meursault looks at the mourners at his mother's home, wondering whether they show "infirmity of age" (Gilbert) or "a nervous tic" (Ward). Finally, the fateful beach outing at the end of the following week shows either ritualistic martyrdom (Gilbert) or temporary insanity (Ward). Camus modulates into a more affective, or emotive, lexicon when Meursault unthinkingly persists in the feud between Raymond and some Arab enemies. When the Arab that Meursault meets holds up a knife, Gilbert chooses the strongest equivalents, suggesting the sun as a divine force. Where Camus continues uninterrupted, Gilbert starts a new paragraph: "A shaft of light shot upward from the steel, and I felt as if a long, thin blade transfixed my forehead. At the same moment all the sweat that had accumulated on my eyebrows splashed down on my eyelids. . . . Beneath a veil of brine and tears my eyes were blinded; I was conscious only of the cymbals of the sun clashing on my skull, and, less distinctly of the keen blade of light flashing up from the knife, scarring my eyelashes, and gouging into my eyeballs." Ward, keeping Camus's paragraphing, chooses weaker terms for physical disorientation: "The light shot off the steel and it was like a long flashing blade cutting at my forehead. At the same instant the sweat in my eyebrows dripped down over my eyelids. . . . My eyes were blinded behind the curtain of tears and salt. All I could feel were the cymbals of sunlight crashing on my forehead and, indistinctly, the dazzling spear flying up from the knife in front of me. The scorching blade slashed at my eyelashes and stabbed at my stinging eyes."

For the climactic ending of part 1, the translators maintain their separate levels of rhetoric. Meursault remembers that, after the fatal first shot, he shot four more times at the inert corpse. Gilbert: "And each successive shot was another loud, fateful rap on the door of my undoing." Ward: "And it was like knocking four quick times on the door of unhappiness."

It is not surprising that translators have had difficulties finding accurate correlatives for Camus's words in other languages. Meurseult is an enigmatic figure whose emotional dimensions are hard to translate. His sphinxlike quality was captured by actor Marcello Mastroianni in the 1967 film version of the novel.

Part 2, which telescopes Meursault's incarceration and trial, features a more thoughtful Meursault. Punishment, as he understands it, means deprivation. When Camus uses the problematic French word *ennui*, Gilbert interprets with "privation" while Ward stays with the more cautious "annoyance." Meursault is roused from his lethargy by the visit of the chaplain, who wants him to repent. When he wakes up later in the night, he thinks of his mother and feels open to the "benign" (Gilbert) or "gentle" (Ward) "indifference of the universe." In the final sentence, Camus indicates the hypothetical nature of Meursault's last wish by putting four of the five verbs in the subjunctive mode. Gilbert, though, uses the conditional mode to show Meursault's sense of mission: "For all to be accomplished . . . all that remained to hope was that on the day of my execution there should be a huge crowd of spectators and that they should greet me with howls of execration." Ward retains the subjunctive and the sense of strangeness it imparts: "For everything to be consummated . . . I had only to wish that there be a large crowd of spectators on the day of my execution and that they greet me with cries of hate."

When Meursault's character changes—as it does when one goes from Gilbert's translation to Ward's—the plot changes, too. Both translations transmit a flawed colonial society that scapegoats a nonconformist, but only in Ward's is it clear that Camus's speaker never realizes that he is a murderer.

SOURCES FOR FURTHER STUDY

Rose, Marilyn Gaddis. *Translation and Literary Criticism*. Manchester, UK: St. Jerome Publishing, 1997.

Reader's Guide to Major Works

THE STRANGER

Genre: Novel
Subgenre: Confession (first-person narrative)
Published: Paris, 1942
Time period: Late 1930s
Setting: Algiers

Themes and Issues. The changing social context of *The Stranger* has brought about a change in readers' perspectives and hence interpretations. In the late 1930s in Algiers, a Frenchman who killed a knife-wielding Arab could probably have been acquitted. Meursault, the murderer, however, thwarts social expectations so much that he is due to be executed as the narrative ends. As Meursault presents the events, he was found guilty because of his likability, sincerity, and indifference. Readers from 1950 through 1960 tended to find Meursault an appealing scapegoat. After Camus's death, his works were much less read. In the late 1980s, when postcolonialism appeared in literary criticism, *The Stranger* was picked up again. Camus's genial presentation was decried; his sincerity and indifference were seen as excuses for callous evasion. The trial, far from a travesty of justice, indicates that, barring the issue of capital punishment, there is a just outcome—perhaps in spite of the author.

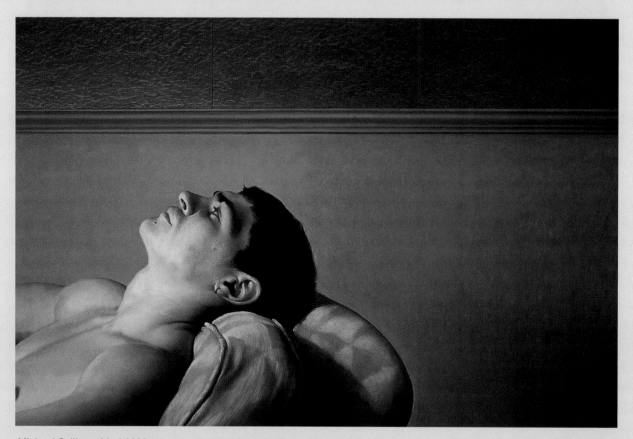

Michael Sell's untitled 2000 artwork suggests the solipsism of Meursault in *The Stranger*. Mired in indifference, trapped in a world of his own moral construction, he can find little emotional attachment to the external elements of his life. As with the figure in the painting, Meursault is lost in self-absorption. Shadows obscure the scene, constantly threatening clarity. At the end of the novel, on the eve of his execution, Meursault declares, "for the first time, in that night alive with signs and stars, I opened myself to the gentle indifference of the universe. Finding it so much like myself—so like a brother, really—I felt that I had been happy and that I was happy again."

DRAMA

1936 Révolte dans les Asturies (Revolt in Asturia)

ESSAYS

1937 L'Envers et l'Endroit (The wrong side and the right side)
1939 Noces (Nuptials)
1942 "The Myth of Sisyphus"
1951 The Rebel
1954 L'été (Summer)
1957 "Reflections on the Guillotine"
1960 Resistance, Rebellion and Death
1963 Notebooks 1935–1942
1966 Notebooks 1942–1951
1968 Lyrical and Critical

1986 Between Hell and Reason: Essays from the Resistance Newspaper Combat, 1944–1947
1986 Neither Victims nor Executioners
1987 American Journals

FICTION

1942 The Stranger (L'étranger)
1947 The Plague (La peste)
1956 The Fall (La chute)
1957 Exile and the Kingdom (L'exil et le royaume)
1972 The Happy Death (La mort heureuse)
1976 Youthful Writings (Écrits de jeunesse)
1994 The First Man (Le premier homme)

1944 Caligula
1944 The Misunderstanding (also translated as Cross Purposes) (Le malentendu)
1948 The State of Siege (L'etat de siège)
1950 The Just Assassins (Les justes)
1960 The Possessed (Les possédés)

The Plot. In part 1, which covers a little more than a week, Meursault, an office worker in Algiers, learns on a Thursday in June that his mother has died at a nursing home 50 miles away. He takes off from work and, at the home, meets her friends at the wake and takes part in the funeral. During the weekend he begins a liaison with a secretary named Marie and gets involved with Raymond, a pimp in his apartment building. In the week that follows, he turns down a promotion to the Paris office and agrees to marry Marie. His demeanor has been pleasant, but throughout, his attitude has been noncommittal; he spares himself even the hint of strong feelings. Then, the following Sunday, on a beach outing to a cottage belonging to Raymond's friends, Meursault, Raymond, and their host are accosted by Arab enemies of Raymond. After a second encounter Meursault, armed with Raymond's gun, goes out walking and finds one of the Arabs. The Arab flashes a knife, and Meursault fires. The first bullet fells the Arab, but Meursault shoots four more times. He realizes he has changed his life.

Part 2 begins after the arrest and covers more than a year. Meursault is questioned closely by officials and his lawyer. He stands trial and is sentenced to death by public beheading. He is convicted, as the prosecutor puts it, "of burying his mother with crime in his heart." Whereas part 1, while narrated in the past, appeared to be taking place soon after narration, part 2 is reconstructed, with hindsight mixed in, in nearly present scenes, until the final chapter when Meursault has a battle of wills with the prison chaplain. With death imminent, Meursault is roused to strong emotion and grabs hold of the priest's cassock to shout about death and absurdity. Later, his face filled with starlight, he thinks about his mother tenderly, as if his rage had washed him clean. He feels happy in a universe as indifferent to his fate as he is and looks forward to death in front of a jeering crowd.

Analysis. If Meursault had lived in the south of France and had shot a fellow Frenchman, it would be easy to follow the prosecutor's argument that someone with such atypical reactions is a menace to society. It could probably be plea-bargained down to manslaughter, given the extreme harshness of the summer day, which it could be said reduced Meursault's ability to think coherently.

The insertion of a colonist-Arab feud muddies the analysis. Raymond beat his Arab girl-friend (whom a letter Meursault wrote for him had lured back to his apartment) so brutally that other French neighbors called the French police. The first encounter on the beach probably involved one of the girl's brothers. It functioned as a reprisal in any case, eliciting an aborted raid by Raymond and Meursault and finally the fatal, one-sided duel. Up to this point there is an underlying metaphor of colonists and revolutionaries, but once Meursault is arrested, interest in the corpse, considered as a former human being, vanishes. It is of interest only because it received four superfluous bullets. At this point the novel's metaphor becomes the dehumanizing effect of colonialism. That is, society uses Meursault's murder as an excuse to eliminate an unfeeling nonconformist. The person he killed does not matter. Therein lies the insidiousness of Camus's letting Meursault be sympathetic: a man who never expresses remorse or regret but just feels bothered. Thus, a fiction originally considered humanistic has become antihuman with the passage of time.

SOURCES FOR FURTHER STUDY

Bloom, Harold. *Albert Camus's "The Stranger."* Philadelphia: Chelsea House, 2001.

Bronner, Stephen Eric. *Camus: Portrait of a Moralist.* Minneapolis: University of Minnesota Press, 1999.

King, Adele. *Camus, "L'Etranger": Fifty Years On.* New York: St. Martin's Press, 1992.

THE PLAGUE

Genre: Novel
Subgenre: Chronicle
Published: Paris, 1947

Time period: Unspecified year in the 1940s, from April 16 to the following February
Setting: Oran, Algeria

Themes and Issues. Often compared to one of its sources, Daniel Defoe's *A Journal of the Plague Year* (1665), *The Plague* debates the place of evil in the universal scheme. Evil is embodied in the bubonic plague, which moves into the Algerian port city of Oran (population 300,000) and causes suffering and death, eliciting both self-sacrificial and self-serving conduct from the inhabitants. On an allegorical level, Camus intended a close parallel with the last 11 months of the German occupation of France during World War II. The Algerian city itself was isolated from July 3, 1940, when the British bombarded the French fleet there, to August 10, 1943, when the Allies took it over.

The Plot. The plot of *The Plague* is as carefully crafted as a medical record. Part 1, April 16 to 30, chronicles the outbreak. It is noticed that rats are dying in suspect circumstances. Dr. Rieux sends his wife to a sanatorium out of the city and has his mother come to keep house. His own concierge dies. Once the cases of individual physicians are added up and analyzed, a senior physician identifies the cause, and ultimately authorities, who did not want to alarm the public, declare an epidemic and close the city.

Part 2, continuing through May until the end of June, gathers together Dr. Rieux's team of plague fighters (all exceptionally well characterized): Grand, a civil servant writing a novel; Rambert, a journalist; Tarrou, a professional revolutionary; and Paneloux, a Jesuit priest. Inasmuch as local authorities have organized prayer days as well as health services, in mid-May Father Paneloux gives the keynote sermon in the city cathedral; he says that plagues have been God's punishment throughout history and that they show God's love.

Part 3 is a very short description of the population's reconciliation to living with the plague, exacerbated in virulence by the summer heat. Part 4, the longest in the novel, illustrates the effects of the plague routine, the sense of exile, and the discrepancy between the disease and justice. At the end of October, the medical team is ready with a vaccine. It is used on a desperate case, the son of Judge Othon. The vaccine, although it will prove a boon, in this first instance delays death but increases the child's suffering. Father Paneloux, a witness to this dying, gives another sermon. Speaking as "we" rather than "you," he advises learning what one can from the plague but not trying to understand it. Who can say, he muses, whether an eternity of joy will compensate for an instant of pain. A few days later the priest dies without most of the usual plague symptoms and is labeled a "doubtful case."

The next month, November, the plague plateaus, and in December, Grand, thanks to the treatment, recovers. Part 5 begins January 25. The plague is declared over, although the city will remain closed for another two weeks. On January 29 Rieux and his mother are tending to Tarrou, who is fatally ill, when they receive word that Rieux's wife has died at the sanatorium. In February, as Rieux watches the celebrations in the street, he reveals his identity as keeper of the record and concludes with a now-famous remark: "He knew what those jubilant crowds did not know . . . that the plague bacillus never dies or disappears for good; . . . and that perhaps the day would come when, for the bane and enlightening of men, it would rouse up its rats again and send them forth to die in a happy city."

Analysis. *The Plague* is a novel where there is something thoughtful to underline on nearly every page. Basically, each comment by Rieux or his coworker Tarrou speaks to the need for human leaders to take over the job of betterment in the absence of God. Rieux tells Tarrou

Dr. Rieux, played by William Hurt in a still from the 1992 film adaptation of *The Plague,* passes a tense and pensive moment. In the novel Camus subjects his characters to deep isolation and ever-widening circles of imprisonment. They are trapped by their own ailing bodies, their pestilential city, and their own dire fate.

early that "if he believed in an all-powerful God, he would cease curing the sick and leave that to Him." The plot bears out this direct humane activism. For example, Paneloux the priest collapses when life contradicts his orthodoxy; Judge Othon's sense of justice is destroyed (and he himself dies later) after his son's ordeal with the trial vaccine; Grand, Rambert, and Tarrou find that service for others outweighs self-fulfillment. Yet Rieux is left with only his dedication and his self-effacing mother. He vows to bear witness to human endurance and concludes that "in time of pestilence there are more things to admire in men than to despise."

Devoid of violence and sex, this novel has other omissions as well. There are no women or Arabs in the team, although there are females among the victims. Except for some blockade runners with Hispanic names, only French Algerian males from some echelon of the middle class participate. In the poorer quarters, where there is poor sanitation, there are more victims. It was fortunate for them that the plague burned itself out. Changing times have made the novel seem myopic and, to certain sensibilities, racist.

SOURCES FOR FURTHER STUDY

Judt, Tony. *The Burden of Responsibility: Blum, Camus, Aron, and the French Twentieth Century*. Chicago: University of Chicago Press, 1998.

—. *Past Imperfect: French Intellectuals, 1944–1956*. Berkeley: University of California, 1992.

Kamber, Richard. *On Camus*. Belmont, CA: Wadsworth, 2001.

THE FALL

Genre: Novelette
Subgenre: Confession (first-person narrative)
Published: Paris, 1956
Time period: 1940s and 1950s
Setting: Amsterdam (with flashbacks to Paris and Algeria)

Themes and Issues. The narrator of *The Fall* examines motives; specifically, doing good deeds for selfish reasons. Through this garrulous narrator, who has stopped doing anything except forcing people to confess to him, Camus asks whether sincerity coupled with inertia is preferable to private kindness and social activism performed with self-satisfaction. In terms of literary history, *The Fall* is Camus's answer to the Marxist-existentialist critics of his essay "The Rebel." In terms of his personal life, it is likely a veiled confession to the world at large that he is not like the saintly Dr. Rieux in *The Plague*.

Plot. Barely 90 pages, *The Fall* is a one-sided dialogue dominated by a man calling himself Jean-Baptiste Clamence (that is, John the Baptist calling in the wilderness). Clamence, formerly a Paris lawyer specializing in noble causes, now holds forth as a judge-penitent in Mexico-City, a bar in a seedy section of Amsterdam. (As a judge he hears and rules on confessions; as a penitent, he makes his own confessions.) In the first chapter Clamence sights a potential penitent and more or less arranges to see him again. In chapter 2, he tells about awakening in disgust with his cleverness and good reputation intact despite his craving for and mindless pursuit of sex. His awakening began with jeering laughter from no discernible source. Chapter 3, which continues with complacent self-criticism, moves from a humiliating traffic encounter with a motorcyclist to an even more complacent description of his abuse of women, including an episode two or three years before his awakening when he failed to rescue a young woman who jumped in the Seine and then called for help. In chapter 4, while showing the interlocutor some sites of tourist interest, he continues with his strong desire for punishment from his peers. In chapter 5, he relates his self-punishment through debauchery. In chapter 6 he says that, when he was imprisoned in Algeria during the war on the charge of collaboration, he was elected a judge by fellow prisoners. He is a self-appointed judge-penitent, and to clinch the appointment he is a fence for a panel, *The Just Judges*, stolen from the Van Eyck brothers'

On one hand, the loquaciousness of *The Fall*'s Jean Baptiste Clamence is a form of self–exposure, the way he is able to present and construct himself to the world. Conversely, true apprehension of his character becomes obscured through his welter of words. Like the figure in Egon Schiele's *Male Nude with Red Cloth* (Graphische Sammlung Albertina, Vienna, Austria), Clamence reveals himself at the same time he hides.

painting *The Mystical Lamb* (1426). As the narrative ends, the narrator waits for his interlocutor, also a Parisian lawyer, to begin. As for wishing that the young woman will throw herself into the Seine again and provide another opportunity for heroism, Clamence says, "It will always be too late. Fortunately!"

Analysis. *The Fall* is a translation of *La chute,* a term the French use for the fall of Adam and Eve. The title thus alerts readers to the religious allusions that are scattered through the narration—generally to put readers off the track. The narrator, who says he has spent 30 years loving himself exclusively, constantly pontificates. Yet inasmuch as he takes pride in his lucid self-criticism, his pontification is contaminated—and he knows it. Camus relies on his readers' common sense to see that each pontification still contains at least a half-truth. For example, Clamence says that all men are judges, all men are guilty, each a Christ in his own way, each crucified without knowing it. Unlike the teammates in *The Plague,* who felt they had to step in because God did not, Clamence believes he can play God for his own gratification. In the end *The Fall* becomes a negative moral metaphor, showing the social risks of both trying to be exemplary for the wrong reasons and taking refuge in superior, prideful self-criticism.

SOURCES FOR FURTHER STUDY

Davison, Ray. *Camus: The Challenge of Dostoevsky.* Exeter, UK: University of Exeter, 1997.

Jones, Rosemarie. *Camus, "L'Etranger" and "La Chute."* London: Grant and Culler, 1980.

Other Works

EXILE AND THE KINGDOM (1957). Published the year of the Nobel Prize, *Exile and the Kingdom* is a collection of six novellas, varying in length from 25 to 50 or so pages. "The Adulteress" is about a woman accompanying her husband on a business trip in North Africa. "The Renegade," the only narration in the first person, is about a defrocked priest who tends the fetish of a pagan salt-mining tribe in the African interior. The tribesmen have cut out his tongue, so presumably he cannot speak. Yet the last line reads, "A handful of salt silenced the babbling slave." In "The Mute" unsuccessful strikers become mildly disoriented when their boss's daughter falls ill and is taken away in an ambulance. "The Guest" (its French title, *L'hôte,* can mean both "host" and "guest") is the most often cited. Daru, a schoolmaster in the French North African interior is asked to hold an Arab prisoner and deliver him to authorities in the next town. Hostile to this policy, Daru offends the soldier who delivers the Arab. He treats the Arab as a guest and takes him to the crossroads. The Arab, whether bound by hospitality or determined to take revenge, deliberately chooses the road to jail. When Daru returns, he finds a note on the blackboard promising vengeance. Like Camus and his Algerian policy, "in this vast landscape he had loved so much, he was alone." The protagonist in "Jonah" is a talented painter who, unable to create once he is famous and beset by publicity, goes berserk. "The Stone That Grows" reflects an excursion to an Afro-Brazilian site during Camus's tour in July and August 1949. A French engineer, D'Arraste, somewhat disoriented in the Brazilian interior, gains acceptance from people regarded as semipagan when he takes part in and passes their initiation ceremonies.

THE FIRST MAN (1994). Camus was working on *The First Man* at the time of his death; it consisted of 144 handwritten pages and a typescript made by his wife. His daughter, who brought the project to publication, added some material from his notebooks. It might have been Camus's final epic statement of the situation in Algeria for the French. Like his parents, the French are simply there when they might

Like the figure in Robert Indermaur's *At the Border II,* Camus's protagonists walk a line between competing or conflicting realms. They are at the center of a struggle between consciousness and perception, guilt and absolution, the truthful and the absurd.

have been somewhere else. The book begins with Camus's own birth and his attempts to reconstruct his parents' early life and continues through his education with flash-forwards to the present of the early 1950s.

THE HAPPY DEATH (1971). Camus's family published *The Happy Death* despite his refusal to pursue publication during his lifetime. Written before *The Stranger,* its 10 chapters are linked by a hedonistic character named Meursault, who also appears in *The Stranger.* Like Camus, Meursault lives in an exclusively European Algiers and visits Prague. In the first chapter Meursault kills Zagreus, a disabled World War I veteran, and steals his savings, yet in the fourth chapter Zagreus veritably invites Meursault to kill him. Whichever murder is the fantasy, Meursault's money problems are solved somehow. Attractive to women and cats, Meursault lives aimlessly but succumbs shortly to tuberculosis.

THE MISUNDERSTANDING (1944). Despite Camus's lifelong interest in the theater and drama productions, his nine plays have had limited success in English. Still, *The Misunderstanding* (also translated as *Cross Purposes*), while rarely performed, has been studied for dramatizing the ambiguities of existentialism. Developed from a newspaper clipping found by Meursault in *The Stranger,* it takes place in a gloomy rural inn of Bohemia. A mother and daughter, who want to escape to a sunny seaside, murder clients for their cash. Jan, their last victim, who is the son of the older woman, wants to surprise his mother and sister and take them away. They are deaf to his hints, however, and avoid opportunities to learn his identity. When they learn whom they have poisoned in poisoning Jan, they decide to commit suicide. They rebuff Jan's wife, who arrives the next day. Alone on stage, the mother falls to her knees in prayer. She asks the servant to help her. Hitherto mute, he replies in a clear, firm voice, "No!"

Resources

Commonly used search engines such as Google or Ask Jeeves will list multiple Camus entries, as will the annual *PMLA* bibliography. Alas, whatever the country of the scholar, most materials are in French.

The Camus Studies Society (http://webcamus.free.fr), which has affiliates in the United States and Japan, offers materials and annual colloquia only in French. It is nonetheless a superb resource and well worth investigating.

Nobel-Related Press Coverage. The popular press extensively covered Camus's Nobel Prize in November 1957 and his death in January 1961. Many of the stories filed at that time can be accessed via microfilm and at large public and university libraries, some of which even have on-line archives. In some libraries bound volumes of periodicals, including major newspapers and newsmagazines, are available for research or casual reading.

Web sites in English. The cupboard is not entirely bare for the Anglophone student, as these three excellent sites make clear (http://www.imagination.com/moonstruck/clsc40.html);(http://www.geocities.com/Athens/Aegean/1311/camus.html); (http://www.levity.com/corduroy/camus.htm).

MARILYN GADDIS ROSE

Alejo Carpentier

BORN: December 26, 1904, Havana, Cuba
DIED: April 24, 1980, Paris, France
IDENTIFICATION: One of Cuba's most important intellectual figures of the twentieth century, Carpentier is best known for his interesting contribution to literary style, the *real maravilloso*.

SIGNIFICANCE: Alejo Carpentier is considered part of the generation of the 1920s, which included writers who came of age after World War I; that generation was also influenced by the triumph of the Russian Revolution and the Marxism-Leninism of its leaders. During that period Latin American nations were trying to modernize but in the process endured political and economic turmoil. In his work Carpentier attempted to highlight the political and cultural currents that he considered appropriate to Latin America through the use of *real maravilloso,* a reality-deforming technique that made the real seem marvelous and the marvelous, real. Carpentier was active in politics, another field in which he made important contributions.

The Writer's Life

Alejo Carpentier was born on December 26, 1904, in Havana, Cuba. His father, Jorge Julián Carpentier, was a French architect, and his mother, Lina Valmont, was a Russian language instructor and pianist. Both decided to leave Europe, convinced of its decadence and enthusiastic to join in the construction of a new country in Cuba. Carpentier's father was also a music lover; this and other interests of his parents would come to influence his life work.

Youth. At the age of 12, Carpentier could play complicated piano pieces, but he never considered himself a musician. His mother guided his musical inclinations, while his father guided his literary studies, and both made up for the gaps in his education at the new Havana schools. In 1913 young Alejo took his first trip to Europe and visited his parents' countries of birth. He studied for three months in France, where he strengthened his French-language skills. Although he did some writing in French, he never felt completely at home in the language.

When his family returned to Cuba, they settled on a ranch outside Havana, where Carpentier enjoyed nature and read extensively. There he also first discovered the harsh

Dancers perform in a rural Cuban village. The move to the ranch outside of Havana proved fruitful to Carpentier's development as a writer. The budding author was exposed to the rich blend of cultures that comprised Cuban society. As a novelist he believed that the universal lay in the local and the regional and that culture was not necessarily a national, but rather a local or site-specific, construction.

Havana was a cultural capital in the first half of the twentieth century. Carpentier once wrote that the city had created its own unique "style devoid of style." For him, Havana was a mass of columns, a continuous colonnade connecting the port with the outlying districts.

reality that the Cuban peasant endured. In 1917 he entered the Instituto de Segunda Enseñanza, where he studied music theory; he also began to write at this time. His family moved again in 1920, to Loma de Tierra, even further removed from Havana. About that time he decided to follow in his father's footsteps, and he eventually went to study architecture in Havana. While he was there, his parents separated, an event that saddened him greatly. He left his architectural studies in 1922.

Formative Years. Carpentier dedicated himself to journalism, which he pursued on and off throughout his life. He saw the beginning of the so-called vanguard movement (a twentieth-century artistic movement with an interest in renewal and exploration, both cultural and

social) and in 1923 joined the Grupo Minorista, a small circle of men with similar intellectual, social, and political concerns. Though many of these men considered themselves communists, most were not active party members. The group advocated a complete change in Cuba's artistic and social values. At 19 Carpentier was the youngest member of the group, which greatly influenced his intellectual formation. The group saw the need to recover an authentic Latin American reality and, at the same time, to remain open to the European aesthetic vanguard.

Carpentier developed a deep interest in the black population of Cuba and studied and participated in its customs and rituals and in the mingling of Catholicism with traditional African religions (a process that scholars term *syncretism).* The syncretist idea of a dimension of mystery pervading and transforming everyday reality appealed greatly to Carpentier, and he strove to absorb as much of this cultural outlook as he could. This interest later contributed to the tone and content of his best-known novels. Along with the influence of his European parents—which was itself mixed with the social environment of colonial Spaniards and African transplants—and his interest in and study of Latin America, his enthusiasm for syncretist ways of thinking helped him develop the concept of *real maravilloso,* a fundamental part of his creative method.

Literary Career Begins. In 1924 Carpentier began to participate in the Movement of Veterans and Patriots against Corruption. He was accused of being a communist and jailed for his activities in 1927. He began his first novel while in prison. Freed in 1928, he fled to Paris. There he collaborated on several journals and hobnobbed with contemporary artists and writers from France. Contact with the French surrealist artists influenced his work, though he never considered himself a surrealist. He did not feel he could contribute to an already mature movement and eventually distanced himself from it.

Paris offered him the intellectually fertile ground he needed for the development of his creativity. While there, the Cuban journal he was working for was banned by the Machado regime in Cuba, and so he turned to radio. He became an important figure in politically oriented radio and worked with Poste Parisien and Radio Luxemburg. He was also editor in chief of the journal *Imán,* through which he met the Chilean poet Pablo Neruda.

Around this time Carpentier decided to learn more about Latin American literature and began reading as many of its classics as he possibly could in order to better understand his own continent. His first trip to Spain was made upon publication of his first book, *Ecué-Yamba-O,* in 1933. There he met contemporary Spanish writers and discovered a love for a country he would visit often. Also in 1933 he married Margarita Lessert, who died soon after from a lung illness.

Carpentier returned to Havana in 1936 for a brief visit, but the political climate and his established life in Europe took him back to Paris. In 1937, during the Spanish Civil War, he participated in the Second International Conference of Writers in Defense of Culture in Spain, where he met again with his writer friends to discuss the impact of the war. He decided

Carpentier's fiction is rooted in his own conceptions of history and time. For him, the human condition was primarily consistent and eternal. He wrote, "Humankind has constants that relate the men of today with men who lived in many various millenniums."

HIGHLIGHTS IN CARPENTIER'S LIFE

1904 Alejo Carpentier is born on December 26 in Havana.

1913 Travels to Europe; studies for three months in Paris.

1921 Begins architecture studies at Havana University.

1923 Joins Grupo Minorista.

1927 Is jailed for communist activity and freed after several months.

1928 Flees Cuba for Paris.

1933 Visits Spain for the first time; publishes *Ecué-Yamba-O;* marries Margarita Lessert, who dies soon thereafter.

1941 Marries Lilia Esteban.

1945 Moves to Venezuela.

1949 Publishes *The Kingdom of This World* in Mexico.

1953 Publishes *The Lost Steps* in Mexico.

1958 Publishes *War of Time* in Mexico.

1959 Returns to Cuba after the revolution.

1962 Publishes *Explosion in a Cathedral* in Mexico.

1964 Publishes volume of essays *Tientos y diferencias;* is honored by José Martí National Library for intellectual work.

1969 Publishes *Literatura y conciencia política en America Latina* (Literature and Political Consciousness in Latin America).

1974 Publishes *Reasons of State* and *Baroque Concert* in Mexico; is honored in Cuba on his 70th birthday.

1975 Is named an honorary doctor by the University of Havana; is awarded the Alfonso Reyes International Award and the Cino del Duca Prize.

1978 Publishes *The Rites of Spring* in Mexico.

1979 Publishes *The Harp and the Shadow* in Mexico.

1980 Dies in Paris on April 24.

to return to Cuba in 1939, both because he missed it and because the political climate in Europe was worsening with the onset of World War II.

In 1941 Carpentier married Lilia Esteban, who became his constant companion and collaborator. In Cuba he continued to engage in journalistic writing and wrote *Music in Cuba* (1946), which was published in Mexico. Though Cuba offered Carpentier a much-needed sense of home, it was not an environment conducive to a literary life. He settled in Venezuela in 1945.

Venezuela. In Caracas Carpentier was able to write more steadily than he ever had before. For him, Venezuela epitomized Latin America. Such important works of Carpentier's maturity as *The Kingdom of This World, The Lost Steps, The Chase, War of Time,* and *Explosion in a Cathedral* were written in Venezuela, though some of these books were first published elsewhere.

Carpentier worked as a radio broadcaster and taught at both the Fine Arts School and the Central University of Caracas. In 1954 he was named director of the J. A. Lamas Institute for his contributions to music. The many trips Carpentier made within Venezuela profoundly influenced his work. After the 1959 Cuban revolution, a brief trip to Cuba convinced him to move back; he was 55 at the time.

Later Years. Carpentier traveled extensively throughout the world as a Cuban cultural ambassador. He taught at the University of Cuba and continued writing and publishing. He also served as underdirector of culture for the Cuban government, vice president of the Union of Writers and Artists, executive director of the Cuban national publishing house, and cultural attaché to the Cuban embassy in Paris, among other positions.

He never refused any political post his country offered him, and when necessary, he went without sleep to continue writing and publish-

Carpentier was influenced by his travels in Venezuela and throughout Latin America. His novels explore unchartered regions—such as the vast expanse in this detail of Tòmas Sanchez's *Laguna Que Espera*—where clarity and certitude are compromised. Logic is replaced by the violation of expectation, and perspective is sometimes skewed.

ing. France, Spain, and Cuba awarded him numerous prizes and honors for his literary work; in addition, he got an award for his political contributions to Cuba. On April 24, 1980, Carpentier died in Paris. In accord with his last wishes, his remains were buried in Cuba.

The Writer's Work

Alejo Carpentier was active in many different fields throughout his life, though they were all closely related. He began to write newspaper articles at a young age and continued to work in journalism throughout his life. He used the writing style he learned as a journalist as a method of approaching unfamiliar situations and literary environments, preparatory to integrating them into an overall narrative. (He was aware, however, that a good writer had to separate the free-flowing pen of journalism from the more taxing demands of literary narrative, or else he would fall into the trap of writing mediocre novels.) Carpentier was also an important force in the field of radio. As a host and an announcer, he helped give form and substance to vanguard radio, which was a force to be reckoned with in the Paris of the surrealists.

Carpentier's literary work also extended into poetry, plays, and essay writing. Though he worked in verse, he thought of it more as text to be set to music than poetry in the strict sense. He wrote two plays for the theater and one for operatic production; he considered all of them worthless without the music that was intended to accompany them. He is, however, best known for his complex novels. He was convinced that the novel must situate the reader in a collective reality and confront the biggest problems of the time. This belief also underlay his work in politics. While he wanted very much to contribute to literature and thought it was an important pursuit, he saw his primary duty as the betterment of his fellow humans through his political activity. Thus, he had many periods of relative inactivity with respect to literature,

during which he dedicated himself to political endeavors.

Perhaps the major contribution of Carpentier to literature was his notion of the *real maravilloso,* which simply means the "marvelously real." This term has been equated with *realismo mágico,* or magical realism. Some critics consider both strategies one and the same thing, while others see distinctions between the two. *Magical realism* was a term first coined by the German art critic Franz Roh to interpret post-expressionist painting. He explained that this art was not a copy of nature but an entirely new creation; the painting makes the real appear unreal and the unreal real. Thus, fantasy takes on the matter-of-course quality of the everyday. The realism of primitive Latin American literature, when mixed with the many magical elements of the mythical and the intuitive, makes reality surprising. It makes the reader marvel.

Many post–World War I Latin American authors, in an effort to describe what they thought

Some critics see Carpentier's writing as a direct response to and tacit dismissal of European surrealism. Yet elements of another literary and intellectual movement, existentialism, creep into his novels. The protagonist in his 1956 novel, *The Chase,* is alone in his plight, pursued and persecuted by an unnamed political force. His sacrifices for his cause are to no avail.

Carpentier's earliest inspiration came from his parents. His father nurtured his love of literature and architecture, while his mother nurtured his love of music and languages. Both immersed him in multicultural environments, an important factor in his formation. His early readings of the French and Russian classics, as well as his later readings of the classics of Latin America, heavily influenced his subsequent literary work. His reading of Latin American literary classics was undertaken in an effort to find his own true Latin American identity. The reading enabled him to develop his own style.

When Carpentier was about 19, he joined the Grupo Minorista, a gathering of young intellectuals who considered themselves in the minority in Cuba because they held leftist views. Some joined the Communist Party. He was the youngest member of this group, and it solidified his political ideology. When he fled to Paris after his first incarceration, he spent a great deal of time with the intellectuals of the surrealist movement, led by André Breton. He was deeply affected by the surrealist attempt to show the absurdity of perceived reality, but he also criticized surrealism for putting completely unrelated objects together in a "forced" magic, that is, a bureaucratic vision of the marvelous that was not founded in reality. Still, surrealism matured Alejo's ideas of how to create and helped him move beyond the folkloric dimensions of his early work to aspects of Latin American life he had not before noticed. He was also influenced by reading the psychoanalysts Sigmund Freud and Carl Jung, both of whom also influenced the surrealists.

Another major influence in Carpentier's life was travel. Traveling and studying in France afforded him an opportunity to polish his French while bringing him closer to his parents' heritage. Later, a trip to Haiti ignited the spark that would set his best work into motion; in this "land of the marvelous," he developed his notion of magical realism. His journey along the upper Orinoco River in Venezuela was also a great influence on his work; the journey revealed to him the true nature of what Latin American reality was. His extended stay as a resident of Caracas solidified his vision of Latin America as complex and contradictory yet surprisingly real. Through contact with nature, he formulated his counter-challenge to surrealism: he would present the real as the marvelous and leave "invention" aside.

A boat plies the waters of the Orinoco River in Venezuela. Carpentier's restless curiosity drove him to explore the reaches of Latin America in an attempt to better understand and represent his world.

of as a new reality, incorporated myth into their work and treated the unreal as a normal part of reality. Thus, while some critics use the terms *realismo mágico* and *real maravilloso* interchangeably, the latter, strictly speaking, is applicable only to Latin American literature. Carpentier describes *real maravilloso* as anything that goes beyond established norms of realism to surprise the reader. The marvelous, however, is not based in someone's imaginings but in reality. It is precisely this firm rooting in reality that differentiates this style from surrealism.

"For what is the history of Latin America but a chronicle of magical realism?" Carpentier wrote in 1949 in the prologue to *The Kingdom of This World,* the first time the term was applied to literature. As in Paul Sierra's 1985 work *Cuatro Santos,* magical realism blurs traditional distinctions between the ludicrous and the horrible, the serious and the comic. Intrigue, romance, and embellishment are featured as well.

A good example of the use of *real maravilloso* in literature is Carpentier's treatment of time. He felt that culture was a form of knowledge that allows one to establish relations beyond time and space, between two realities that are similar even though they might be separated by centuries. For example, many of his characters struggle to be free in time. Carpentier in fact posits two kinds of time, each based on a different reality: Western historical (restrictive) time, from which his characters flee, and African time, where nature and time are one and eternal and represent a state of paradise. This concept of time is very clear in "Journey Back to the Source" and "The High Road of Saint James," two stories in *War of Time.* In "Journey," the main character travels backward through time, from death to birth and then to the womb, where time ceases to be. *The Lost Steps,* another story in the same collection, also centers around the nature of time.

Carpentier uses *real maravilloso* to emphasize many other issues as well.

BIBLIOGRAPHY

Franco, Jean. *An Introduction to Latin American Literature.* London: Cambridge University Press, 1969.

González Echevarría, Robert. *Alejo Carpentier: The Pilgrim at Home.* Austin: University of Texas Press, 1990.

González Echevarría, Robert, and Klaus Müller-Bergh. *Alejo Carpentier: Bibliographical Guide.* Westport, CT: Greenwood Press, 1983.

Janney, Frank. *Alejo Carpentier and His Early Works.* London: Tamesis, 1981.

King, Lloyd. *Alejo Carpentier: His Euro-Caribbean Vision.* Trinidad: Research & Publication Fund Committee, 1972.

——. *Towards a Caribbean Literary Tradition.* Washington, D.C.: Three Continents Press, n.d.

Shaw, Donald Leslie. *Alejo Carpentier.* Boston: Twayne, 1985.

Tusa, Bobs. *Alejo Carpentier: A Comprehensive Study.* Chapel Hill, NC: Albatros Hispanofila Ediciones, 1982.

Reader's Guide to Major Works

THE KINGDOM OF THIS WORLD

Genre: Novel
Subgenre: Magical realism; social criticism
Published: 1949
Time period: 1751–1822
Setting: The Haitian revolution

Themes and Issues. Carpentier first formulates his vision of the *real maravilloso* in the prologue. Characters, ideas, and concerns collide and coincide to make up reality. For example, the concepts of individual and collective liberty are demonstrated through the characters and presented by contrasting the persons and situations of slaves and masters, whites and blacks. Another issue, which also appears in subsequent works, concerns the need of the characters to take revolutionary action, even though it always leads to failure and disillusionment. For these characters, the suffering of one must benefit all.

The Plot. The reader is witness to a series of revolutions for freedom led by black slaves for

Afro-Caribbean religion, depicted here in *Ceremony Cousin Zaka (Voodoo Scene)* by twentieth-century artist A. Pierre, adds to the charged atmosphere of Carpentier's *The Kingdom of This World.* The author's conception of magical realism is first embodied in this novel, in which elements of the fantastic offset the often grim backdrop of rebellion and execution. The competing interpretations of Mackandal's fate embody the tension between the two. At his execution, the ropes binding him suddenly loosen and fall, "and the body . . . rose in the air, flying overhead, until it plunged into the black waves of the sea of slaves. A single cry filled the square: Mackandal saved!" Is he though?

the benefit of other black slaves. The novel begins with Ti Noel's visit to Cabo when he is a boy and continues as he witnesses the lives of three others: Mackandal, Bouckman, and King Henri Christophe. In the first part of the novel, Mackandal learns about black magic and tries to use this and other African traditions to free the slaves. He is eventually executed by the white owners for poisoning a white man; the slaves, however, believe Mackandal has escaped the pyre of death by employing black magic. A particular reality is seen from two different viewpoints: the whites see a dead man, while the blacks see a man transcended.

Bouckman is a black shaman who sacrifices himself for the good of the people. He leads a rebellion against the whites by sowing terror among them. Eventually he is executed, but slavery ends as a result of his rebellion. King Henri Christophe tries to eliminate the rule of the French by adopting their ways and rejecting the customs and traditions of the blacks. When he was made king, he embraced Catholicism and in so doing tried to make the blacks "white." He is shown in sharp contrast with Mackandal and Bouckman; in the end he commits suicide after being paralyzed by a stroke, because both the powers above and the people are working against him.

Ti Noel is the slave of Lenormand de Mezy and must follow him to Cuba when he flees revolutionary Haiti. Mezy's mansion becomes Christophe's when the latter takes over Haiti. Ti Noel is disillusioned by a lifetime of failed revolutions and tries to flee his reality by using black magic to change into an animal. He is unsuccessful and eventually realizes that he must use his powers to serve men and women and not to desert them. In his old age Ti Noel, having gone insane, imagines that he has returned to Haiti, to Christophe's mansion, where he holds royal balls and events. This delusion is his freedom. The novel ends with Ti Noel's disappearance.

Analysis. This novel was born out of a trip to Haiti that provoked Carpentier's rejection of surrealism; the prologue is a critique of surrealism as well as a presentation of the *real maravilloso*. Carpentier displays a piece of Haitian history (Mackandal, Bouckman, and Henri Christophe are historical figures), rigidly following historical facts though departing from a chronological arrangement of events. This approach symbolizes the contradictions the author finds in Latin American reality. Through contrasting and varying perspectives, he presents cultural diversity, conflicts, and combinations.

In this novel the black population is presented as no longer powerless, though the power of the African gods is still evident. Mackandal is a symbol of the human desire to seek freedom, a desire that no repressive society can eliminate no matter how hard it tries. Carpentier also uses the Catholic liturgical year to enrich meaning: Mackandal's uprising begins on Epiphany, and he is transformed at the beginning of the new year. One of de Mezy's wives dies on Pentecost Sunday. This complex book includes numerous examples of magical realism that offer a new vision of Latin American reality.

SOURCES FOR FURTHER STUDY

Harvey, Sally. *Carpentier's Proustian Fiction: The Influence of Marcel Proust on Alejo Carpentier.* London: Tamesis, 1994.

Young, Richard. *Alejo Carpentier: El reino de este mundo.* London: Grant and Cutler 1983.

THE LOST STEPS
Genre: Novel
Subgenre: Magical realism; social criticism
Published: 1953
Time period: 1950s
Setting: Ranges from a New York City museum to the Amazon jungle

Themes and Issues. *The Lost Steps* offers another alternative to European surrealism and was inspired by Carpentier's journey up the Orinoco River in Venezuela. The treatment of time (psychological and physical, Western and non-Western) is a major theme throughout. It depicts the protagonist's search for collectivist forms and structures to alleviate his isolation.

The Lost Steps subverts traditional narrative structure. Instead of a logical progression of events, original intent is altered and for the narrator there is no clear and discernible path before him. The composer, out to research the music of the Orinoco region, actually transforms his conception of his life. This private and unexpected revelation is embodied in Paul Sierra's oil-on-canvas painting *Swimmer #16,* in which the man seems to be emerging into a world he has never seen or experienced before.

this new land and to his new lover, Rosario, a mestiza woman who embodies this new sense of time that he has been seeking.

In this atmosphere the musicologist begins to write a cantata (a choral work) about his contact with nature. His experience leads him to reflect on the absurdity of death. Yet like everyone else, he is condemned to live in historical time. Though Rosario illuminates his trek through the wilderness and the narrator wants to stay with her in this primitive world, he cannot remain because he cannot undo his connection to dates and time.

Analysis. *The Lost Steps* is about the transformation of consciousness, as the narrator's search for native musical instruments turns into a search for roots and meaningfulness. It invites the reader to discover the meaning of the adventure.

The Plot. A New York musicologist is sent by a U.S. university to find examples of musical instruments from the Latin American indigenous population. He leaves behind his estranged wife, Ruth, an actress, and his French lover, Mouche, an intellectual, as he embarks on this life-changing journey. The nameless narrator's path from the debilitating city in the North lands him in the South, where he reaches the mythical point of Santa Mónica de los Venados, a visionary place that spurns the temptations of gold and exploitation. He is drawn to the life outside of historical time that he finds in

Carpentier again uses the Catholic liturgy to enhance meaning in this work. The story begins on Pentecost, a feast commemorating the descent upon the faithful of the Holy Spirit. When the narrator begins his trip back in time, the 15 lampposts of Los Altos illuminate the 15 mysteries of the Virgin Mary celebrated in the rosary. In Spanish, the word for *rosary* is *rosario,* the name of the mestiza lover of the narrator.

SOURCES FOR FURTHER STUDY

Smith, Verity. *Alejo Carpentier: Los pasos perdidos.* London: Grant and Cutler, 1983.

ESSAY COLLECTIONS

1964 Tientos y diferencias
1969 Literatura y conciencia politica en América Latina
1981 The Latin American Novel on the Threshold of a New Century and Other Essays

FICTION

1933 Story of Moons (written in French)
1933 Ecué-Yamba-O
1946 Music in Cuba
1949 The Kingdom of This World
1949 Tristán e Isolda en tierra firme
1953 The Lost Steps
1956 The Chase
1958 War of Time: Three Short Stories and a Novella
1962 Explosion in a Cathedral
1972 Right of Sanctuary
1974 Reasons of State
1976 Chronicles
1979 The Rites of Spring
1979 The Harp and the Shadow
1979 Under the Sign of La Cibeles: Chronicles on Spain and the Spanish
1980 La música que llevo dentro
1982 La ciudad de las columnas

PLAYS

1974 Baroque Concert

POETRY

1930 Two Afro-Cuban Poems
1931 Antillean Poems (written in French)

ALEJO CARPENTIER

THE KINGDOM OF THIS WORLD

TRANSLATED BY HARRIET DE ONÍS

EXPLOSION IN A CATHEDRAL

Genre: Novel
Subgenre: Magical realism; social criticism
Published: 1962
Time period: 1791–1808
Setting: Cuba, Haiti, France, Guadalupe, Cayenne, and Spain

Themes and Issues. *Explosion in a Cathedral* was written after the Cuban revolution and Carpentier's return to Cuba in 1959. It deals with the integration of the worldviews Carpentier separates into the categories female and male, where the female represents timelessness and the mystical and the male represents action. These themes unite in a total vision of reality and repeat concerns voiced in other works: ideals are lasting, but human actions to put them into motion ultimately fail, and a man always chooses action over the mystical, in spite of the temptation to do otherwise.

This novel is a retelling of *The Kingdom of This World* on a broader scale; here the issues are no longer mutually exclusive and form an integrated whole. It also takes up issues in *The Lost Steps* by illuminating the path to integration with the timeless female absolute, always desired but never attained. The central characters are Sofía, Esteban, and Víctor; Esteban and Víctor sharply contrast with one another, and Sofía functions as the balance between the two

.

The Plot. Sofía and Carlos's father dies and leaves three children. Sofía returns to care for her brother and her sickly cousin, Esteban. Víctor Hugues visits Sofía and impresses her with his new ideas; he also cures Esteban with the help of a mulatto, Oyé. Sofía is thereby freed of the duty of being caretaker and becomes Hugues's lover. Hugues leaves the island with Esteban to travel in search of adventure, and Sofía, feeling abandoned, marries and settles for a bourgeois life she does not really want.

When Esteban and Hugues return, Sofía's husband dies of a mysterious fever. Sofía, in spite of Esteban's declaration of love for her, returns to Hugues and goes to Cayenne with him, while Esteban, desperate, confesses to revolutionary subversion and is imprisoned. His confession gives Sofía and Víctor time to escape. In Cayenne, Sofía discovers that, though Víctor at first introduced the principles of the French Revolution and freedom to the New World, he is now reinstating slavery under the orders of Napoleon. She leaves him and goes to Spain to help free Esteban and care for him, as he is again ill.

While in Madrid, Sofía joins in a rebellion, and Esteban follows her; they both die. Carlos then goes to Madrid to find out what he can about their deaths; he discovers nothing and lives out his days uneventfully. Carlos shares many of Sofía's and Esteban's ideals but is content with his life of comfort (he also financially supports them in their adventures). Víctor returns to Haiti to live in relative anonymity.

In Dennis Aufiery's oil-on-canvas painting *Balseros,* bathers gather on a seawall much like the one bordering the Malecon, the boulevard that lines Havana's waterfront. In *Explosion in a Cathedral,* the lives of two men and a woman are woven into a tight net. While on one level, Carpentier develops Esteban, Víctor, and Sofía as three-dimensional characters, they are also types, exemplifying of their genders and revolutionary ideals.

Analysis. The novel is structured along three separate lines: the masculine principle is Víctor Hugues, a man of action with little intellectual framework. Esteban represents a minor theme; his name is that of Saint Esteban (Stephen), the patron saint for those, like the author, born on December 26. The feminine principle is represented by Sofía, whose name is the Greek word for "wisdom." Each character, in a different way, is meant to symbolize the wisdom of the Afro-Cuban heritage of freedom.

Víctor is a chameleon-like creature who embodies eighteenth-century French traditions and establishes the thematic limits of the book—revolutionary hope and inevitable disillusion. Sofía repeatedly chooses action to better humanity. She thinks that, though human beings are weak, they have valid and lasting ideals. She is a courageous idealist whose ideas are based on emotion. Esteban is disillusioned by the repeated failures of revolution, but he is a man of action and does what he can while wrestling with his desire to escape time. He believes that spiritual perfection through the escape of historical time can come only as a collective development of humanity. In the end he sacrifices himself so that Sofía can fulfill her goal.

As in other works, Carpentier employs repetition and contrasts to make his points. The title of the painting that serves as the English title of the book, *Explosion in a Cathedral,* is repeated as a point of reference for the characters (and readers) to measure the extent of their ideological, political, and personal changes and how they deal with the events of their lives. The repetition of phrases is also important. Sofía repeatedly says, "We have to do something!"

Carpentier again follows the Catholic liturgical year closely. Victor arrives at Sofía and Esteban's house on Holy Saturday (when God is dead and not yet resurrected). He embodies evil in the form of action and enters chaotically into the free world of the Cubans. Again, it is Christmas Eve when Esteban realizes he is in love with Sofía and New Year's Day when Carlos arrives to hear how Sofía

and Esteban sacrificed themselves to help others gain freedom.

SOURCES FOR FURTHER STUDY

Gikandi, Simon. *Writing in Limbo: Modernism and Caribbean Literature.* Ithaca, NY: Cornell University Press, 1992.

Webb, Barbara. *Myth and History in Caribbean Fiction.* Amherst: University of Massachusetts Press, 1992.

Other Works

ECUÉ-YAMBA-O (1933). Carpentier did not want to publish his first work, *Ecué-Yamba-O*, because he thought it was obvious in its literary devices though correct in political ideology. He agreed to its publication only to forestall the appearance of pirated versions. Menegildo, the main character, is a young black man drawn irresistibly to criminality. He leaves the countryside for the city, where his life loses the purpose and focus that gave it authenticity, and he strays from the religious traditions of Santería. He becomes an actor in a sideshow and often spends his Sundays at a spiritualist center. There, after a celebration where musicians profane a rhythm sacred to the congregants, he is killed in the resulting violence.

The villagers react to the overwhelming power of the African gods with passive submission and fatalism; the gods' power is all-encompassing and determines the black Cuban's life. Carpentier's earliest description of Afro-Cuban mysticism, this book equates the national with the Afro-Cuban. Militant cultural nationalism is highlighted in a critique of Cuban social structure that offers no opportunity to the Afro-Cuban.

WAR OF TIME (1958). Various aspects of time are the central concern of *War of Time*, a compilation. The most interesting stories are "Journey Back to the Source" and "The High Road of Saint James," which, respectively, show time moving in reverse and in a circular fashion.

"Journey Back to the Source" emphasizes the power of black religion. Melchor, a shaman representing the earth mother (a goddess), prevents the dying Marquis de Capellanías, Marcial, from having a Catholic funeral and going to paradise. Though it is never made clear why, Melchor makes Marcial live his life backward, from death to birth to disappearance into his mother's womb (for Carpentier, a journey toward freedom). In short, Melchor causes him never to have been born. Even Marcial's estate returns to nothingness, to dust.

In "The High Road of Saint James," two ideas—the female as a place of refuge and the male as the impetus to action—are again seen as mutually exclusive. Juan the soldier takes the high road because he has not kept faith with God. His pursuit of his goal leads to destructive action, from which he flees and seeks refuge. His refuge is in stopping time and finding the love and protection of a black woman who cures him. Recurrence—the circularity of time—is the central theme.

In this edition also are "Like the Night" and "The Chosen," and other stories that take up concerns of Carpentier's other narrative works.

REASONS OF STATE (1974). *Reasons of State* is Carpentier's "dictator novel," and some say he wrote it as a sort of parody of the historical style seen in his other works. The protagonist is the President, a dictator of a nameless Latin American country who lives in Paris, his cultured refuge from his homeland. Still, he identifies enough with his roots to return home on occasion to quell uprisings.

An atmosphere of falsity and lies abounds, culminating in betrayal by the President's closest adviser, who disguises himself and escapes after the President's fall from power. When the President dies, he is buried in Paris. The only remaining loyal ones are his black nurse and lover and his mestizo ambassador to France. Even his daughter is indifferent, as he was to her. The President's life was false because he did not trust his people to be free.

When he is overthrown, he is replaced by a professor who promises a new era but is incapable of action. The Student, a revolutionary, leaves the Notre Dame Cathedral in Paris through the door commemorating the resurrection of the dead, an act that sparks hope. Though the novel is full of many historical references, the story is fictitious.

Resources

A wide range of materials concerning Alejo Carpentier and his writings is available to the student. Some of them follow.

Alejo y lo Real Maravilloso (CINED Production Group, 1986), directed by Luis Acevedo Fals. This documentary is in Spanish with no English subtitles. It explains Carpentier's concept of the *real maravilloso* through interviews and dramatized scenes from *The Kingdom of This World*. It outlines Carpentier's life and work through the mid-1970s (www.lavavideo.org).

Capital Community College. This college, in Hartford, Connecticut, has a Latin American Students Association, which offers detailed analyses of several major Carpentier works. Interested students can visit the group's reading room (http//cctc.commnet.edu/stuweb/~perez7511/LASA8.htm).

Faces, Mirrors, Masks: Twentieth Century Latin American Fiction. This series of seven sound recordings was produced by Frieda Werden and directed by Frank Tavares (Washington, D.C.: Instructional Communications Systems of the University of Wisconsin Extension and National Public Radio, 1984). The half-hour programs profile most of the significant writers of Latin America with interviews, dramatic excerpts, music, and on-location recordings to create portraits of the writers as storytellers and social critics.

Latin American Network Information Center (http://info.lanic.utexas.edu) and **Latinworld** (http://www.latinworld.com) are comprehensive search engines on Latin American literature.

Library of Congress Online (http://lcweb2.loc.gov/hlas/hlashome.html) offers an annotated guide to Latin American literary works.

Unión de Escritores y Artistas de Cuba. This Web site is in Spanish only. However, it offers a wealth of information about the organization Carpentier belonged to and supported, as well as information on the Alejo Carpentier Literary Prize (www.uneac.com).

Wisconsin Regional Library for the Blind and Physically Handicapped. Many of Carpentier's works are available on-line through this organization. Plot synopses of *The Chase, Explosion in a Cathedral, The Harp and the Shadow, Kingdom of This World,* and *The Lost Steps* may also be obtained in cassette and disk formats, as well as in braille (www.execpc.com/~wgraczyk/adulta-a.html#carpentier).

LORENA TERANDO

Aimé Césaire

BORN: June 25, 1913, Basse-Pointe, Martinique
IDENTIFICATION: Twentieth-century black French Caribbean poet, playwright, essayist, and statesman, and also one of the founders of the racial pride movement known as negritude.

SIGNIFICANCE: Through a career that spanned eight decades and two hemispheres, Césaire fundamentally changed the accepted wisdom about race and the effects of colonialism. The concept of negritude identifies an international black race that links all blacks of African descent, whether European, North American, South American, Caribbean, or African. This international concept, the first of its kind, had a lasting effect on a wide variety of literary, social, and political movements and essentially invented identity politics. Césaire himself adopted negritude as a working ideal—in his poetry, particularly the early poem *Notebook of a Return to the Native Land;* in his drama, especially *A Tempest* and *The Tragedy of King Christophe;* in his political essays and histories; and in his career in both French and Martinican politics.

Birth and Early Life. Aimé Césaire was born June 25, 1913, in Basse-Pointe on the eastern Caribbean island of Martinique, one of the French Antilles. At that time most nations were either colonial powers or colonial possessions. Martinique was the latter. The official language was French, but most of the population, the descendants of African slaves brought over to work the sugarcane plantations, spoke Creole. Slavery had been abolished in Martinique in the 1840s, but racial and economic injustice continued.

Césaire was the second of six children. His father was a civil servant who realized that, if his children were going to succeed, it would have to be in the world (and the language) of the colonizer not the Creole, and he read to them from the classics of French literature. The young Aimé showed tremendous academic skill; when he was 11, the family moved to the largest city on Martinique, Fort-de-France, the only place where he could be educated beyond grade school. He showed such talent that, even in the competitive French academic system, he distinguished himself and went on to continue his education in France.

Education in France. Césaire arrived in Paris in 1932. Because of the French educational system, where students either qualify or are "weeded out" by the rigorous system of examination, Césaire (who had made it) studied with the very best students. He also met many students like himself, black colonial subjects who had left their homelands for the first time and were thrown into a world very different from the nations in which they had been raised. Césaire had traveled to France with a classmate who was already a good friend: Leon-Gontran Damas, a native of French Guiana in South America. At school he met Léopold Sédar Senghor, who was a native of (and would later become the president of) the West African nation of Senegal and a poet like Césaire. With these friends Césaire founded a small magazine, *The Black Student,* in 1934. It is in this magazine that the word *negritude* first appeared.

By 1935 Césaire had been accepted into the École Normale Supérieure, one of the finest universities in France. There he and his friends read Leo Froebenius, a historian whose *History of African Civilization* had just been translated into French. Froebenius had a great effect on the young men, because he identified in precolonial Africa a noble civilization, an idea to which these French subjects of African descent

The rurality of this residential setting in Basse-Pointe (left), Martinique, where Césaire was born, lies in stark contrast to the urbanity of Fort-de-France (right), the largest city in Martinique, where Césaire's father hoped to give his precocious son an extended and opportune education.

This informal and undated photograph of Césaire shows him standing with three members of the First International Congress of Black Intellectuals and Artists at the Sorbonne in Paris, France, the city where Césaire's perspective on what it means to be a black colonial was forever changed.

had never been introduced. Colonialism, by its very nature, tries to erase all the positive aspects of the cultures it encounters, representing itself as the civilized system that brings civilization to the savage races. Césaire,

Senghor, and Damas had been raised on the idea that the French were superior to them, and to a large extent they adopted that perspective. Froebenius gave them a new pride in their race and fundamentally changed Césaire's

Césaire, a prominent politician on Martinique for more than three decades at the time this photograph was taken, addresses the crowds during Martinique's legislative elections in March 1978.

Martinique with his wife and growing family just as World War II was declared in France. Césaire became a teacher at his old school in Fort-de-France. He continued to write poetry throughout the war and published a journal, *Tropiques,* from 1941 to 1945. He was a very active writer throughout the 1940s and 1950s and published several books of poetry.

Political Life. Césaire, like many intellectuals of his youth, was attracted by the ideas of communism, one of the few systems that offered a critique of colonialism. Many of the ideals of communism can be seen in his writing, particularly his connection of race with class and the role poverty plays in his works as a force that destroys the humanity of those who suffer under it. Césaire was an active communist until about 1956; thereafter his work and political life continued to be informed by a fight for economic and racial justice.

In Martinique, Césaire is better known as a politician than a poet. He has been active in politics in both France and Martinique since the end of World War II

perspective on the colonial relationship. In addition Césaire experienced the literary movement of surrealism, which attempted to rebel against a repressive society and represent real human experience through seemingly disconnected sets of impressions.

Return to the Caribbean. In the mid-1930s Césaire began *Notebook of a Return to the Native Land* after a visit to his homeland. Around this same time he married a fellow Martinican, Suzanne Roussy. In 1939 he returned to

and founded, in the 1950s, the Progressive Party of Martinique. In 1945 he was elected mayor of Fort-de-France, a capacity in which he served for more than half a century. In addition Césaire went to Paris as a representative of the département of Martinique in the French National Assembly after World War II. He opposed independence for Martinique but argued for a commonwealth relationship with France. In the mid-1990s, he gradually decreased his political commitments, while remaining an important public figure.

Césaire has written primarily poetry, drama, and political commentary. In addition he has been a founder or cofounder of several influential magazines, including *The Black Student (L'etudiante noir), Tropics (Tropiques),* and *The African Presence (Présence africaine).* Though he writes only in French, the majority of his works exist in English translation, and he is widely respected worldwide for the complexity and commitment he brings to both literature and politics.

Though he writes in a broad variety of genres, his concerns have been consistent throughout his career: the political and personal effects of colonialism on its subjects. This pursuit includes examinations of the perspective of the colonized subject and the tragedies that inevitably follow decolonization. His work, however, is not preachy; he presents real human emotion in real situations and leaves political conclusions to be drawn by the reader.

Poetry. As a poet Césaire is primarily a surrealist and was recognized by the founder of the surrealist movement, André Breton, as one of the finest practitioners of that form. His poetry is powerful and immediate, using sight, sounds, even smells to evoke for the reader the situation and emotions of the speaker. In doing so, Césaire does not tell the reader about his world, he invites the reader into his world.

Plays. In his dramatic works, Césaire often presents a rebellion, sometimes successful, sometimes unsuccessful, and its aftermath. His dramatic language is more poetic than natural, and his plays tend to re-create specific classical forms. *A Tempest,* for example, directly follows Shakespeare's story line and structure although Césaire reconfigured his characters for the Caribbean context. *The Tragedy of King Christophe* borrows both from the comedy of manners of Moliére and from the classical tragic structure of the Greeks.

Histories and Political Writings. As a historian Césaire writes from the unique perspective of someone who has been defined primarily from the outside: the colonial subject. He forces Western intellectuals to confront the myths upon which colonization was based and in doing so reinterprets Caribbean history.

SOURCES FOR FURTHER STUDY

Arnold, A. James. *Modernism and Negritude: The Poetry and Poetics of Aimé Césaire.* Cambridge, MA: Harvard University Press, 1981.

Césaire, the deputy of Martinique, addresses the colonial members of Parliament on May 8, 1947, at a meeting of protest against the arrest of the deputy of Madagascar.

Davis, Gregson. *Aimé Césaire.* Cambridge, UK: Cambridge University Press, 1997.

Eshelman, Clayton, and Annette Smith. "Introduction." In *The Collected Poetry of Aimé Césaire.* Berkeley: University of California Press, 1983.

Pallister, Janis L. *Aimé Césaire.* New York: Twayne, 1991.

HIGHLIGHTS IN CÉSAIRE'S LIFE

1913   Aimé Césaire is born in Basse-Pointe, Martinique

1924   Family moves to largest city, Fort-de-France; Césaire continues his education at the Lycée Victor Schoelcher.

1932   Moves to Paris to pursue higher education at the Lycée Louis-le-Grand.

1934   Participates in the founding of *L'Étudiante Noir,* a magazine for black students.

1935   Continues his education at the École Normale Supériere. Begins writing *Notebook of a Return to the Native Land,* his first major creative work.

1937   Marries his fellow Martinican Suzanne Roussy in Paris.

1939   First major poem is published. World War II begins on September 1; Césaire returns to Martinique on September 4.

1941   Participates in the founding of the review *Tropiques.*

1945   Becomes mayor of Fort-de-France, Martinique.

1945–1946   Goes to France as a deputy requesting département status for French colonies in the Caribbean; his request is granted March 16, 1946.

1948   Césaire participates in the founding of the magazine *Présence africaine.*

1950   Publishes *Discourse on Colonialism.*

1956   Turns to drama with *And the Dogs Were Silent: A Tragedy;* breaks with the Communist Party in *Letter to Maurice Thorez.*

1976   *Complete Works* published in Fort-de-France.

1984   *Aimé Césaire: The Collected Poetry* nominated for the Los Angeles Times Book Award.

1990   Césaire hosts the International Counsel of Francophone (French-speaking) Studies in Fort-de-France.

2000   Steps down as mayor of Fort-de-France in June.

AIMÉ CÉSAIRE

NOTEBOOK OF A RETURN TO THE NATIVE LAND

Translated and edited by Clayton Eshleman and Annette Smith

With an Introduction by ANDRÉ BRETON

Reader's Guide to Major Works

NOTEBOOK OF A RETURN TO THE NATIVE LAND (Cahier d'un retour au pays natal)

Genre: Lyric poem
Style: Surrealism
Published: 1939, 1956
Time period: 1930s
Setting: Fort-de-France, Martinique

Themes and Issues. The poem presents the perceptions of a Caribbean native returning to his homeland after time abroad. The poem chronicles his transition from seeing his people and homeland as debased and disgusting to seeing them as victims of a degrading colonial power to restoring his own pride in his origins.

Analysis. Césaire's first major poetic work was begun in 1935, restructured several times, and published in its final form in 1956. It is a long poem, a collection of fragments of images, memories, and sensory experiences in order to create a feeling rather than a narrative. The speaking character of the poem is an educated black Antillean returning home from, as the poet says to himself, "Bourdeaux and Nantes and Liverpool and New York and San Francisco." This brief catalog suggests that Césaire is referring not only to himself but also to other young men who, like him, may have gone to England or America instead of France. The poem provides little specific information about the narrator. The empha-

sis of the poem is his perception of his land and its people.

The poem takes place at dawn, on the boundary between night and day; the phrase "at the end of the wee hours" is repeated throughout the poem. There are several rea-

Artist Alfredo Arreguin's 1992 oil painting *Sueno (Dream: Eve before Adam)* reflects a period of universal innocence, a time before cultural identity and true human existence were completely erased from view by colonial imperialism, an atrocity that Césaire writes passionately about in his 1939 lyric poem, *Notebook of a Return to the Native Land,* and his 1950 political essay, *Discourse on Colonialism.*

sons for this repetition. The narrator himself is at a boundary between Europe and the Caribbean, between light and dark, between white and black. Having returned from abroad, he sees his homeland starved, diseased, and in a drunken state. The poet presents a series of striking images: people as human vomit waiting to be spewed up from the slums where they live; a child who cannot learn because he has not eaten and is criticized for being lazy and stupid; a pitiful boxer on the streetcar, beaten by poverty. These images are contrasted with moments of transcendence—the church on Christmas, the history of African nobility, and the Haitian revolution—to create not a story but a set of impressions. These contrasting images identify the problems of his society and place the blame not on the people but on their colonizers, who have broken a noble race. The poem is, as Pallister calls it, "a journal of how Césaire's shame evolved into pride."

This is a very difficult poem. Like Césaire himself and the narrator, the poem exists in two worlds at once. On the one hand it is justly recognized as a classic work of Caribbean literature and a statement rejecting colonial models of political and racial identity. It condemns the colonizers for creating a society with the economic and spiritual poverty that Césaire describes in such detail. On the other hand the poem is a masterpiece of French literature and a crucial text of French surrealism. Thus, Césaire is both criticizing colonialism and using its forms at the same time.

SOURCES FOR FURTHER STUDY

Irele, Abiola, ed. "Introduction." In *Cahier d'un Retour au Pays Natal,* 2nd ed., by Aimé Césaire. Columbus: Ohio State University Press, 2000.

DISCOURSE ON COLONIALISM (Discours sur le colonialisme)
  Genre: Political essay
  Published: 1950

SOME INSPIRATIONS BEHIND CÉSAIRE'S WORK

Césaire was greatly influenced by the lively intellectual climate of Paris in the 1930s, particularly the political movement of Marxism and the literary movement surrealism. Both openly challenged the status quo, making an energetic attempt to re-create their respective fields while doing so. At the same time he was influenced by (and became an influence upon) a close circle of friends, particularly Leon-Gontran Damas and Léopold Sédar Senghor, each of whom became a prominent intellectual figure in his own right. Together, they articulated, defined, and practiced the values of negritude, a concept that fundamentally changed perceptions of race in the twentieth century.

Léopold Sédar Senghor, former president of Senegal, poet, and friend to Césaire for most of his life, poses with one of his books in Tours, France, on May 10, 1985. With Senghor and their mutual friend Léon-Gontran Damas, Césaire originated the concept of negritude, a movement of great influence to restore the cultural identity of black Africans. Senghor wrote some of his finest poetry while he was imprisoned in Nazi concentration camps in the early 1940s, by which time Césaire was fortunate enough to be back in Martinique.

POEMS

1939 Notebook of a Return to the Native Land (originally published in the French journal Volontes; final version published 1956)
1946 The Miraculous Weapons
1948 Solar Throat Slashed
1949 Lost Body
1960 Shackles
1961 Cadastre
1966 State of the Union (translated selections from The Miraculous Weapons, Shackles, and Cadastre)
1982 I, Laminarian
1983 Aimé Césaire: The Collected Poetry (in English and French)
1985 Non-Vicious Circle: Twenty Poems (in English)
1990 Lyric and Dramatic Poetry, 1946–1982 (in English)

PLAYS

1956 And the Dogs Were Silent: A Tragedy
1963 The Tragedy of King Christophe
1966 A Season in the Congo
1969 A Tempest: After the Tempest of Shakespeare

JOURNALS

1934 The Black Student (L'Étudiante Noir)
1941–1945 Tropics (Tropiques)
1948 The African Presence (Présence africaine)

HISTORIES & POLITICAL WRITINGS

1948 Commemoration of the Centenary of the Abolition of Slavery: Speeches Given at the Sorbonne on April 27, 1948 (with Gaston Monnerville and Léopold Sédar Senghor)
1950 Discourse on Colonialism
1956 Letter to Maurice Thorez
1960 Toussaint L'Ouverture: The French Revolution and the Colonial Problem
1978 Culture and Colonization

Themes and Issues. Césaire identifies the three defining aspects of colonization: the violence with which it is established and enforced, the economic bases on which it rests, and the necessary complicity of the population in the colonizing nation. Quoting from numerous European sources on the necessity of colonialism, Césaire shows how the discourses of religion, economics, psychology, and human progress were all united in a racist project to defend colonialism as an inevitable historical force.

Analysis. In his most influential political essay Césaire is fearless about identifying the wrongs of colonialism and placing the blame on all Europeans. No one is innocent who lives in a nation that colonizes other lands. Writing soon after World War II, Césaire evokes the image of Hitler to help European audiences understand the damaging effects of colonialism. For Césaire, Hitler's methods differed very little from those of the European colonizers, but Hitler perpetrated his acts in Europe on white Europeans. At the end of the essay, Césaire considers whether America offers colonized peoples a preferable system, decides no, and calls it "the great Yankee risk." For Césaire, at this time an adherent of communism, the only relief from colonialism would come when a classless society would right the wrongs of the past. The *Discourse* is a deeply principled and emotional criticism of a damaging social structure and is written with an immediacy and passion that makes readers feel as though they themselves are on the receiving end of this system.

SOURCES FOR FURTHER STUDY

Munro, Martin. *Shaping and Reshaping the Caribbean: The Work of Aimé Césaire and René Depestre.* London: Modern Humanities Research Association, 2000.

Other Works

THE TRAGEDY OF KING CHRISTOPHE (La Tragédie du Roi Christophe) (1963). In the 1960s, Césaire turned to the stage, writing three major plays in ten years. The first was *The Tragedy of King Christophe,* set after the Haitian revolution, when the island of Haiti was divided in two parts, one ruled by the president of the Republic, Pétion, and the other by a slave turned general turned king, Henri Christophe. Christophe, who has rejected the presidency, comically mimics the forms of European royalty. As in all classical tragedy, however, Christophe falls victim to his own hubris. He forces his followers to build him a castle, an act that creates resentment and results in his suicide.

A SEASON IN THE CONGO (Une Saison au Congo) (1966). In *A Season in the Congo,* Césaire treated a similar but more contemporary subject: the 1960 revolution in the Congo and its aftermath, focusing on the career of the first Congolese president, Patrice Lumumba, and his assassination the following year. Unlike Christophe, however, Lumumba does not cause his own downfall because of hubris; he is the victim of his own subordinates.

A TEMPEST (Une Tempête) (1969). *A Tempest* is a retelling of Shakespeare's drama about a shipwreck that throws European noblemen onto a deserted island inhabited only by a man they had wronged and sent into exile and his daughter and servants. Here it is restructured as a colonial narrative, with Prospero represented as a power-hungry tyrant and Caliban as the rebellious slave and as a figure for the colonized native.

Resources

Aimé Césaire: A Voice for History (1994). Césaire is the subject of this three-part videotape documentary (*Aimé Césaire: un voix pour l'histoire*) by the internationally acclaimed director Euzhan Palcy. It is distributed by California Newsreel (http://www.newsreel.org).

CUNY-Lehman College in New York City has a site that is only in French, but it features some useful links to other Césaire sites and so is worth the extra trouble that using it might entail (http://www.lehman.cuny.edu/ile.en.ile/paroles/cesaire.html).

Other Web Resources. Most Web sites on Césaire have been designed by professors at universities for the use of their students; some of them are very useful for general readers, too. One excellent introductory site is located at Emory University (http://www.emory.edu/English/Bahri/Cesaire.html).

MARY E. DONNELLY

Chou Shu-jen

BORN: 1881, Shaoxing, Zhejiang Province, China
DIED: 1936, Shanghai, China
IDENTIFICATION: Early-twentieth-century Chinese writer and social critic.

SIGNIFICANCE: Chou Shu-jen, better known by his pen name, Lu Xun (or Lu Hsün), was a leading literary figure of early-twentieth-century China. He is probably best known for two collections of short fiction written between 1918 and 1926. These short stories examine a variety of social topics and are among the earliest examples of modern fiction in China. Lu Xun's writings are characterized by a sharp critique of the feudal legacy of traditional Chinese culture and society and a sensitivity to social injustice, as well as by a profound sense of loneliness. Although he never joined the Communist Party, Lu Xun was increasingly interested in leftist thought and literature during the last decade of his life. Shortly after his death he was effectively canonized by the leader of the communist revolution, Mao Zedong.

The Writer's Life

Chou Shu-jen (whose name is also spelled Zhou Shuren) was born in 1881 in Shaoxing, in Zhejiang Province. While the name he was given at birth was actually Zhou Zhangshou, he has become best known by his pen name, Lu Xun (or Lu Hsün), and he is seldom referred to by any other name. Most celebrated for his short stories, Lu Xun was a remarkably eclectic and prolific writer who also published a volume of lyric poetry, and several volumes of literary criticism and translations, as well as a vast collection of acerbic, short essays (known as *zawen* in Chinese). Lu Xun was one of the leaders of the early-twentieth-century modernization movement in China and was also closely involved with the growing Chinese leftist movement in the late 1920s and early 1930s.

Childhood and Family Background. Lu Xun was born into an illustrious family of the gentry class, although it was already on the decline. His paternal grandfather had passed the highest rung of the competitive civil service examinations and received the *jinshi* degree. His father, however, never managed to receive any degree above the lowest, the *xiucai* degree, and later in life tended to smoke opium and drink to excess.

At the age of 11, Lu Xun was sent to the school run by the Zhou clan, where he studied the traditional fare of the Chinese classics, a course that would have prepared him to follow in his grandfather's footsteps. A year later, in 1893, however, his grandfather was imprisoned for taking bribes while administering the same civil service examinations to which he had owed his own success. This event plunged Lu Xun's family into poverty and disgrace. A year later, in the winter of 1894, Lu Xun's father fell ill; he died in 1896. Lu Xun was convinced that his father's death was as much a result of the blunderings of his doctors (who prescribed an assortment of ineffectual traditional remedies) as it was a result of the disease itself (probably tuberculosis, the same disease that would claim Lu Xun's own life 40 years later).

Lu Xun (above) had a childhood laced with tragedy. When he was thirteen, his grandfather, accused of bribery, was imprisoned for what would be seven years. Each fall the family had to offer bribes themselves, sending money to the Ministry of Punishment to be sure their grandfather was not executed. This overtly corrupt system tainted Lu Xun's view of the traditional ways and goaded him to embrace eventually more revolutionary ideals.

Education. In 1898, two years after his father's death, Lu Xun enrolled in the Jiangnan Naval Academy in Nanjing. Rather disenchanted with the curriculum, he transferred to the School of Mining and Railways of the Jiangnan Army Academy a year later. There he was exposed to the popular "new learning" movement, which included a large component of texts and ideas derived from the West.

Upon graduation in 1902, Lu Xun was sent to Japan on a Chinese government scholarship. After spending two years studying Japanese, he transferred to the remote city of Sendai to spend a year and a half studying medicine at the Sendai Medical School. As he later described in the preface to his first collection of fiction, his decision to abandon his medical studies was precipitated by a disturbing experience he had one day in class. After the regular lecture was finished, the professor showed some images from the ongoing Russo-Japanese War. One slide depicted the public execution by the Japanese of a Chinese man accused of spying for the Russians. More than the execution itself, what struck Lu Xun about this image were the apparently apathetic expressions of the other Chinese spectators, who had presumably been brought in by the Japanese to observe the execution.

This seminal moment convinced Lu Xun that China's real problem was more spiritual than physical and therefore that if he hoped to help China, he needed to go home to try to cure his countrymen's souls rather than stay in Japan to learn how to cure their bodies. Though Lu Xun stayed in Japan for the next few years, he enthusiastically threw himself into this project of social reform (with only limited success, however).

The revolution brought great changes to Lu Xun's nation. Here a group performs exercises under the watchful eye of Mao Zedong at a re-education camp northeast of Peking.

Returning to China in 1909, Lu Xun spent the better part of the next decade as more or less a recluse. Having temporarily abandoned his earlier aspirations for social reform, he devoted much of his time and energies to the esoteric study of classical texts.

The May Fourth Movement. Lu Xun resumed his politically engaged writings around 1918, on the eve of the May Fourth Movement, a term that refers to the Chinese student protests of the provisions in the Treaty of Versailles (May 4, 1919), which officially concluded World War I, and by extension to the various attempts at social and cultural reform in China from the mid-1910s through the 1920s. The goals of these reformist movements included introduction of Western thought and culture into China, abolition of conservative ideas and values, equalization of the sexes, and increased democratization of literature.

Lu Xun's was one of the most prominent and influential voices in the May Fourth Movement. He was sharply critical of the ways in which specific dimensions of China's traditional culture were currently contributing to its relative weakness as a nation. Lu Xun was also concerned with the question of whether

Chinese writings were too difficult for the common people to understand. In fact, he spearheaded the movement to use the contemporary vernacular in new writing instead of the hard-to-read classical Chinese in which most texts up to that point had been written.

The Leftist Period. After the nearly simultaneous completion in 1926 of his second volume of stories and his collection of prose poems, Lu Xun made an explicit decision to shift from creative writing to more direct political engagement. During the final decade of his life (1926–1936), Lu Xun wrote quite prolifi-

cally but mainly in the format of the polemical short essay, or *zawen*.

After 1926 Lu Xun became increasingly involved with leftist and socialist organizations in Shanghai and elsewhere, notably the influential League of Left-Wing Writers. As a consequence, he came into contact with many aspiring writers and artists. By all accounts he was extremely supportive of younger writers and artists.

Posthumous Developments. Already quite influential by the time he died in 1936, Lu Xun's reputation truly blossomed during the decades that followed. In 1940 the future

In the 1920s and 1930s Chinese fiction assumed greater dimensions of social criticism. Some authors embraced revolution. Their writing took on propagandistic elements and was concerned more with ideology than with the portrayal of realistic characters or the inner workings of human nature. Other writers were unsure of what direction to take and simply turned to chronicling the everyday plight of China's most underprivileged citizens. Lu Xun, depicted in a painting above, eschewed both of these approaches. In his writing, he presented slightly exaggerated figures and put them in scenarios that transcended the political realities of his times. In this way, his stories became timeless analogies that universalized some of the anguish his characters personified.

In the works of Lu Xun, sympathy and nostalgia tug against a call for change and a clear-eyed endorsement of a radically changed future. This uneasy duality is evident in the author's own relation to his past. Of his childhood, he wrote, "When I was young I, too, had many dreams. Most of them I later forgot, but I see nothing in this to regret. For although recalling the past may bring happiness, at times it cannot but bring loneliness, and what is the point of clinging in spirit to lonely bygone days? However, my trouble is that I cannot forget completely, and these stories stem from those things which I have been unable to forget."

founder and chairman of the People's Republic of China, Mao Zedong, praised Lu Xun in almost hagiographic terms: "The chief commander of China's cultural revolution, he was not only a great man of letters but a great thinker and revolutionary. Lu Hsün was a man of unyielding integrity, free from all sycophancy or obsequiousness; this quality is invaluable among colonial and semicolonial peoples." Given this extraordinary endorsement, it is hardly surprising that Lu Xun has become a literary phenomenon in contemporary China and remains lionized in both critical and popular circles.

There are three separate editions of Lu Xun's complete works, ranging from 8 to 20 volumes. In addition, there are 2 supplemental volumes, a 24-volume collection of his diaries, and countless other primary and secondary works detailing every facet of his life and work. There have been 15 literary and art journals (many still in print) devoted exclusively to his life and work. Furthermore, the largest and most elaborate museum in China devoted to a single author is the beautiful and well-funded Lu Xun Museum in Shanghai. In sum, Lu Xun has enjoyed an unrivaled level of popular and critical adulation in mainland China.

The Writer's Work

Lu Xun's reputation as the father of modern Chinese literature is grounded on something of a paradox. Although the standard 1981 edition of his collected works contains 16 volumes and more than 8,000 densely packed pages, Lu Xun's reputation as a creative writer is nevertheless based largely on two modest collections of short stories, together with a third volume of prose poetry. In fact, with the exception of "Remembrance of the Past," which he wrote in 1911, all of Lu Xun's fictional writing dates from the eight-year period between 1918 and 1926. This relatively modest corpus of stories, however, conceals an impressive range of literary style and subject matter.

Early Idealism. Lu Xun began writing while still in Japan. There, between 1907 and 1908, he wrote several philosophical essays in an exceedingly dense and difficult version of classical Chinese. One essay, "The Power of Mara Poetry," takes the Nietzschean figure of the transcendental superman and uses it as a model for social critique. The vocabulary of this essay is so difficult (even for native Chinese readers) that there is a heavily annotated edition that "translates" the essay into a more readable version of contemporary vernacular Chinese.

Between Past and Present. The linguistic difficulty of Lu Xun's Japan-period essays

As in Hung Liu's 1995 work *Five Eunuchs,* the writings of Lu Xun capture a clash between traditional and contemporary China. This struggle is evident in the author's introduction to his 1935 short-story collection *Old Stories Retold.* In it he writes, "In some places the narrative is based on passages in old books, elsewhere I gave free rein to my imagination. And having less respect for the ancients than for my contemporaries, I have not always been able to avoid facetiousness."

HIGHLIGHTS IN CHOU'S LIFE

1881	Chou Shu-jen is born in Shaoxing, China.
1887	Enters a traditional school run by his own family.
1896	His father dies.
1889	Chou goes to school in Nanjing; adopts the name Chou Shu-jen.
1902	Goes to Japan on a government scholarship.
1904	Studies medicine in Sendai.
1906	Abandons his medical studies and returns to Tokyo.
1906	Returns briefly to Shaoxing to marry his fiancée, Hu'an; returns to Tokyo a few months later.
1909	Returns to China from Japan.
1918	Publishes "Diary of a Madman" in the journal *New Youth.*
1923	Publishes *Call to Arms,* his first collection of short stories.
1926	Leaves Beijing for Shanghai.
1927	Arrives in Guangzhou (Canton), where he accepts position as professor of Chinese at Zhongshan University.
1928	Founds the literary journal *The Torrent* with Yu Dafu.
1929	Son, Hai Ying, is born.
1930	Chou joins League of Left-Wing Writers.
1932	Begins to be plagued by numerous physical problems.
1936	Dies in Shanghai from tuberculosis.

is noteworthy, since later one of Lu Xun's explicit goals was the creation of a more intelligible vernacular version of classical Chinese. His 1918 short story "Diary of a Madman" is often regarded as one of the first works of Chinese literature to be written in the vernacular. Later in his life, Lu Xun even suggested that Chinese ideographs (characters) be abolished altogether and replaced with alphabetic transliterations.

Many of Lu Xun's views are informed by the ideological radicalism that characterized much of the May Fourth Movement. In particular, Lu Xun was critical of arranged marriages, mandatory chastity of widows, and such traditional Chinese schools of thought as Confucianism, Taoism, and Buddhism. At the same time, however, Lu Xun was very interested in traditional Chinese literature and culture. Much of his intellectual energy during his period of reclusion (1909–1918) was devoted to the study of classical texts. Furthermore, his modestly entitled *Brief History of Chinese Literature* (published in two volumes) constituted an important and largely unprecedented attempt to treat Chinese fiction as a worthy subject of serious scholarly examination.

Movement to Darkness. Recurrent in Lu Xun's writings is his critique of what he saw as the Chinese national character. In "Diary of a Madman," he identifies this collective flaw as

in "Diary of a Madman," the execution scene at the end of "The True Story of Ah Q," the son's being eaten by a wolf in "New Year's Sacrifice," and Kong Yiji's horrific beating in "Kong Yiji." Similarly, "Forging the Swords" features a macabre scene of three decapitated heads trying to devour one another.

In his prose-fiction collection *Wild Grass* these themes are developed most explicitly. This profoundly dark and macabre work is virtually without parallel in modern Chinese fiction.

Western philosophy, particularly the writings of Friedrich Nietzsche, helped to shape Lu Xun's evolving perceptions of the relations between politics and literature. The struggle would never be fully resolved and would plague him throughout his literary life. "I have always felt that literature and politics are often in mutual conflict," he wrote in his essay "Literature on the Eve of Revolution." "The purpose of politics is to maintain the status quo, and naturally it points in a direction different from literature, which is not satisfied with the status quo. . . Politics seeks to maintain the status quo in order to consolidate it, whereas literature prompts society to progress and gradually detaches it [from politics]."

metaphorical cannibalism, while in "The True Story of Ah Q" and "Kong Yiji," he identifies it as a sort of perverse self-delusion.

In the preface to his short story collection *Call To Arms*, Lu Xun describes how his decision to focus on writing derived from his viewing of a wartime slide of a Chinese prisoner being beheaded. Similar scenes of death and mutilation continued to haunt many of his subsequent works: the fantasy of cannibalistic consumption

BIBLIOGRAPHY

Chen, Shuyu, et al., eds. *A Pictorial Biography of Lu Xun.* Beijing: People's Fine Arts Publishing, 1982.

Chen, Pearl Hsia. *The Social Thought of Lu Hsun, 1881–1936.* New York: Vantage, 1976.

Foster, Paul. "Lu Xun, Ah Q, 'The True Story of Ah Q' and the National Character Discourse in Modern China." Ph.D. diss., Ohio State University, 1996.

Hsia, C. T. *A History of Modern Chinese Literature.* New Haven, CT: Yale University Press, 1960, pp. 28–54.

Hsia, Tsi-An. *The Gate of Darkness: Studies on the Leftist Literary Movement in China.* Seattle: University of Washington Press, 1968.

Kowallis, Jon. *The Lyrical Lu Xun: A Study of His Classical-Style Verse.* Honolulu: University of Hawaii Press, 1996. Includes English translations of many of Lu Xun's classical poems.

Lee, Leo Ou-fan. *Voices from the Iron House: A Study of Lu Xun.* Bloomington: Indiana University Press, 1987.

—, ed. *Lu Xun and His Legacy.* Berkeley: University of California Press, 1985.

Lyell, William A. *Lu Hsün's Vision of Reality.* Berkeley: University of California Press, 1976.

Semanov, V. I. *Lu Hsün and His Predecessors.* Translated by Charles Alber. New York: Sharpe, 1980.

Wang, Shiqing. *Lu Xun: A Biography.* Beijing: Foreign Languages Press, 1984.

Chou and the New Woodcut Movement

It is one of the great ironies of modern Chinese literary history that Lu Xun, commonly identified as the father of modern Chinese literature, saw fit to dedicate a considerable portion of his energies during the last five years of his life (1931–1936) to the nonliterary Chinese New Woodcut Movement. An enthusiastic participant in virtually every facet of this movement, Lu Xun not only promoted the movement itself but also encouraged young artists, amassed a large personal collection of Chinese and foreign woodcuts, oversaw the publication of many collections of woodcut illustrations, and designed the wood-block cover art for his own books and those of others. In addition, he was, to a more limited extent, a graphic artist in his own right.

In contrast with the vast amount of scholarship that has been dedicated to Lu Xun's literary works, little serious attention has been given to his involvement in the graphic arts. Although most literary studies duly make note of his woodcutting endeavors, there is often the general implication that these nonliterary accomplishments were not truly worth the time spent on them by a man of such genius.

Although Lu Xun's work with the Chinese woodcut movement was concentrated in the 1930s, whereas the bulk of his more conventional literary work was completed in the late 1910s and early 1920s, the roots of both of these interests can, by one reckoning, be traced to the year 1918. That was both the year that Lu Xun wrote and published his seminal "Diary of a Madman" and the year that he started to collect foreign woodcut illustrations to serve as potential pieces of cover art for the literary journal *The Torrent,* which he had just founded that year.

It is fair to say, however, that Lu Xun's involvement with the visual arts was already evident long before this moment in 1918. His interest in woodcut printing, for instance, apparently began in boyhood with a fascination for illustrated fiction. When he was in primary school, he was fond of tracing illustrations from classic Chinese novels, such as *Suppressing Bandits* and *Journey to the West.* Furthermore, Lu Xun consistently maintained this concern throughout his adult life, as suggested, for instance, by diary entries that record the large number of art books he purchased. Given this lifelong interest in the graphic arts, particularly in traditional Chinese wood-block illustrations, Lu Xun's "return" to these issues in what would turn out to be the last years of his life is better seen as a sort of homecoming to his own youthful predilections.

In addition to marking a point of return within Lu Xun's own biographical trajectory, the Chinese New Woodcut Movement also constituted a return to a centuries-old technology that was originally invented and developed in China. As Lu Xun himself emphasized in countless essays, the New Woodcut Movement was grounded on a return to a technology that had very old and deep roots in China. Woodcut printing in China dates from as early as the eighth cen-

In essence, it can be said that Lu Xun started his life and ended his life with his love affair for Chinese woodcuts, such as the 1947 Chinese woodcut seen here, *Scramble for Rice,* by woodcut artist Chao Yen-niem. The woodcut captures the desperation of people rioting for rice, a result of the shortage of food caused by hoarding and profiteering.

tury, whereas in Europe the technology was not developed until about 600 years later, in the fourteenth century.

The use of wood-block printing as an art form reached its peak in China around the sixteenth and seventeenth centuries, with the widespread production of high-quality, exquisitely detailed, and multicolored illustrated texts. By the nineteenth century, however, the technology was primarily being used as a cheap way of producing a large volume of low-quality printings. It was precisely at this time, moreover, that European artists had started to make wood-block printing an art form in its own right. It is therefore ironic that Lu Xun and his colleagues should turn first to European wood-block printing for inspiration on how to re-develop this ancient Chinese artistic and technological practice.

Lu Xun's interest in woodblock printing can also be seen in the context of his views on the democratization of literature. Wood-block prints of images and written texts could be produced cheaply. Furthermore, the visual nature of the prints allowed for information and emotions to be conveyed, via graphic images, to viewers who might not be fully literate. Finally, the inherent "roughness" of many wood-block prints gave them a more common or proletarian feel, which undoubtedly fit in well with Lu Xun's political sympathies during his last years.

SOURCES FOR FURTHER STUDY

Hsia, Tsi-an. *The Gate of Darkness: Studies on the Leftist Movement in China.* Seattle: University of Washington Press, 1968.

Reader's Guide to Major Works

PREFACE TO *CALL TO ARMS*

Genre: Essay
Subgenre: Autobiographical sketch
Published: 1923
Time period: 1900s through 1910s
Setting: Japan and China

Themes and Issues. The preface to *Call to Arms* is a retrospective essay that outlines the evolution of Lu Xun's attitudes toward social engagement. It details his frustrations with outmoded traditional practices (including the use of folk medicine, which, he contended contributed to his father's death) and with the perceived political and moral apathy of the Chinese people as a whole. The essay describes Lu Xun's ultimate decision to use fiction as a tool to heal and reform China's national spirit.

Contents. This influential essay provides many insights into Lu Xun's views on the writing of fiction. Written in 1923, this preface to Lu Xun's first collection of short stories presents a quasi-autobiographical account of the events that led up to his decision to write "Diary of a Madman" (the first story in the collection). It contains moving discussions of the author's childhood experiences while caring for his sick father, his subsequent years in Japan studying medicine, and his years of disillusionment following his return to China. A memorable moment in the essay is his account of having viewed, in one of his microbiology classes in Japan, a wartime slide of a Chinese prisoner being executed by the Japanese. Lu Xun recalls that it was actually his disgust with the apathetic expressions on the faces of the

A family of refugees flees from an embattled land. Images of people rendered helpless, those around them blind to the need of their fellow citizens, stirred Lu Xun and added a social and revolutionary fervor to his writing. Through his powerful images of individuals caught in desperate situations, Lu Xun hoped to enact social change.

SOME INSPIRATIONS BEHIND CHOU'S WORK

Lu Xun lived and wrote during a period of rapid and profound change in China. He was, therefore, acutely aware that Chinese ways appeared weak and "diseased" in comparison with those of the West. As a result, most of his writings were concerned with pinpointing and critiquing the various factors that contributed to China's national weakness.

Even as Lu Xun was critiquing the influence of tradition on contemporary society, he remained deeply interested in traditional Chinese literature and culture. In a 1936 collection, *Old Stories Retold,* for instance, Lu Xun strategically rewrites a number of traditional stories to make them more relevant to contemporary concerns. Throughout his life Lu Xun also remained fond of writing poetry in a deliberately antiquarian style.

As he was developing as a writer, Lu Xun took inspiration from a number of Russian, European, and Japanese writers. He was long interested in the nineteenth-century German philosopher Friedrich Nietzsche, whose works Lu Xun not only translated into Chinese but also frequently alluded to in his own writings. Later, leftist movements and Marxist aesthetics affected his thinking markedly, although he never formally joined the Chinese Communist Party.

Chinese spectators in the picture that led him to decide to devote his energies to reforming the Chinese national character.

Analysis. This essay not only presents Lu Xun's own explanation and rationalization of what he attempted to accomplish through his fiction but provides important insights into some of the ambivalencies and tensions that continued to haunt his work throughout the rest of his career. In this essay he first presents his famous sketch of the "iron house" metaphor. Specifically, Lu Xun suggests that China may be compared to an iron house that is in flames, with all of its inhabitants asleep inside, trapped and oblivious of the impending disaster. Lu Xun asks whether it would not be better simply to allow the inhabitants to perish quietly in their sleep rather than attempt to wake them and run the risk of having them suffer a much more painful demise. Ultimately he decides that the risk is a reasonable one, and he sets out to write "Diary of a Madman" as a first attempt to awaken his fellow countrymen to the disaster confronting them.

SOURCES FOR FURTHER STUDY

Chow, Rey. *Primitive Passions: Visuality, Sexuality, Ethnography, and Contemporary Chinese Cinema.* New York: Columbia University Press, 1995, pp. 4–18.

"DIARY OF A MADMAN"

Genre: Short story
Subgenre: Modernist social critique
Published: 1918
Time period: Early twentieth century
Setting: Unspecified

Themes and Issues. In "Diary of a Madman" Lu Xun develops his famous critique of the "cannibalistic" nature of traditional Chinese society. Drawing loosely on social Darwinist notions popular at the time, Lu Xun suggests that the "evolution" of Chinese society has basically remained stalled at the level of reptiles. The "mad" narrator is increasingly fearful for his own personal safety, even as he implicitly engages with broader concerns about the health and ultimate fate of Chinese society in general.

The Plot. Partly inspired by the Russian writer Nikolai Gogol's short story of the same title, this tale is told in the voice of a narrator who becomes convinced that his neighbors—and even his immediate family—are all secretly cannibals and are scheming to eat his flesh. As the narrator's fears grow, he becomes certain that his own fate is sealed and that everyone around him, in fact, is locked into a cycle of cannibalistic consumption. The famous last lines of the story nevertheless articulate a glimmer of hope: "Perhaps there are still children who have not yet eaten men. Save the children."

The short preface of the story postdates the events narrated in the diary itself and suggests an ironic contrast to the conclusion of the actual story. The preface is written in the voice of an old friend of the diarist, who is given the diary by the diarist's brother. The reader finds out that the madman himself was subsequently "cured" and went on to take a position as a government official.

Analysis. "Diary of a Madman" is often regarded as China's first modern short story. Beyond its critique of traditional culture, one of the qualities that helps it earn this designation is that most of the story is written in the modern vernacular version of Chinese (that is, the language that people use when actually speaking to each other) rather than in the archaic written Chinese that had been used in fiction and other writings up to that point. The preface of the story, by contrast, is written in the more difficult classical language.

This story stands as a transparently allegorical critique of traditional Chinese society and culture. The madman's madness, therefore, should actually be seen as a brief moment of lucidity, whereby he becomes aware of the social realities to which those around him remain blind. The madman's subsequent "cure" is therefore highly ironic in that he has lost his momentary insight into the social ills around him and has himself succumbed to the more

---

SHORT STORIES

1911 "Remembrance of the Past" ("Huaijiu")
1918 "Diary of a Madman" ("Kuangren riji")
1919 "Kong Yiji" ("Kong Yiji")
1919 "Medicine" ("Yao")
1921 "Hometown" ("Guxiang")
1921 "The True Story of Ah Q ("Ah Q zhenzhuan")
1924 "New Year's Sacrifice" ("Zhufu")
1924 "Upstairs in a Wineshop" ("Zai jiulou shang")
1924 "Soap" ("Feizao")

COLLECTIONS

1923 Call to Arms (Nahan)
1926 Wandering (Panghuang)
1936 Old Stories Retold (Gushi xinbian)

POETRY

1927 Wild Grass (Yecao)

ZAWEN ESSAY COLLECTIONS

1924 The Grave (Fen)
1925 Hot Air (Refeng)
1926 Unlucky Star (Huagai ji)
1927 Unlucky Star, part 2 (Huagai ji xubian)
1928 And That's That (Eryi ji)
1932 Three Leisures (Sanxian ji)
1932 Two Hearts (Erxin ji)
1933 Book of False Freedom (Wei ziyou shu)
1934 Quasi-Romance (Zhun fengyue tan)
1934 Mixed Accents (Nanqiang beidiao ji)
1935 Anthology of Unanthologized Works (Jiwai ji)

1936 Fringed Literature (Huabian wenxue)
1936 Essays Written in a Semi-Concession (Qie qieting zawen)
1936 Essays Written in a Semi-Concession, part 2 (Qie qieting zawen erji)
1936 Essays Written in a Semi-Concession, part 3 (Qie qieting zawen mobian)

LITERARY CRITICISM AND OTHER ESSAYS

1924 A Brief History of Chinese Fiction, part 1 (Zhongguo xiaoshuo shi lue)
1925 A Brief History of Chinese Fiction, part 2
1928 Dawn Blossoms Plucked at Dusk (Zhao hua xi Shi)

In "Diary of a Madman," cannibalism becomes a potent and visceral emblem of the lives consumed by an oppressive feudal system. It is too late for the Madman to save himself, but not too late, in the story's famous last line to "Save the children," typified here in a detail from *Innocence,* Chin-Cheng Hung's pastel on paper. Some scholars argue that cannibalism has literal, in addition to symbolic, importance in the story. In his essay "Fan Ainong," Lu Xun writes of an actual case of cannibalism and the elements of savagery that had infiltrated the fringes of Chinese society.

pernicious social "disease" of "cannibalism." His subsequent accession to a position as a government official similarly should be taken as an indication not so much of his successful reintegration into "normal" society as of the degree to which it was precisely the Confucian nature of the state bureaucracy that contributed to this cannibalistic disease in the first place.

SOURCES FOR FURTHER STUDY

Sun Lung-kee. "To Be or Not to Be 'Eaten': Lu Xun's Dilemma of Political Engagement." *Modern China* 14, no. 4 (1986): 459–485.

"MEDICINE"

Genre: Short story
Subgenre: Social critique
Published: 1919
Time period: 1910s
Setting: Unspecified

Themes and Issues. Set against the background of a poor couple trying to help their son, who is dying of tuberculosis, "Medicine" returns to Lu Xun's critique of the popular use of ineffectual folk remedies instead of modern Western medicine. The story also expresses sympathy with the unnamed and largely invisible revolutionary who has just been executed when the story opens (and whose blood the parents purchase in order to feed it to their son).

The Plot. This story focuses on a young boy who is dying from tuberculosis. His parents, in desperation, decide to try an old folk remedy, that calls for feeding the boy human blood. The father therefore attends the execution of an accused revolutionary and succeeds in obtaining some of the dead man's blood. The boy's parents then soak a *mantou* bun in this blood and feed it to their son. He dies soon after, despite their efforts. The final scene of the story takes place in the cemetery, where the mother of the boy and the mother of the executed revolutionary have gone to visit their sons' graves.

Analysis. The emphasis in "Medicine" on the use of the blood-soaked bun as a cure for tuberculosis can be compared with Lu Xun's scathing critique, in the 1923 preface to *Call to Arms,* of

In the preface to *Call to Arms* as well as in the story "Medicine," Lu Xun did not hide his disgust at Chinese herbal medicine practices. The writer argued that China needed a "spiritual medicine," rather than a remedy for the physical ailments of its people. In blindly holding on to superstitions and outmoded methods, it was the family, especially rural clans such as the one pictured here, that was suffering.

traditional folk remedies that he felt were ultimately responsible for his father's death.

The ending of this story is significant. The two mothers are surprised and confused by the wreath of flowers that has mysteriously appeared over the revolutionary's grave. Whether it was placed there by supernatural powers or by secret sympathizers of the revolutionary's cause, the wreath is a sign of hope. As with the call to "save the children" at the end of "Diary of a Madman," this hopeful note at the end of "Medicine" may seem somewhat out of context within the story as a whole. Lu Xun singled out this cemetery wreath as an example of the use of a literary technique he called "bent pen," which consists of closing on a deliberately optimistic note specifically to lift readers' spirits.

SOURCES FOR FURTHER STUDY

Dolezelova-Velingerova, Milena. "Lu Xun's 'Medicine.'" In *Modern Chinese Literature in the May Fourth Era*, edited by Merle Goldman. Cambridge, MA: Harvard University Press, 1977, pp. 221–232.

"THE TRUE STORY OF AH Q"

Genre: Short story
Subgenre: Social satire
Published: 1921
Time period: Late 1900s and early 1910s
Setting: Unspecified

Themes and Issues. Lu Xun's longest work of fiction and one of his best known, "The True Story of Ah Q" centers around the unforgettable character Ah Q, whose misplaced pride, social obtuseness, and general stupidity are generally seen as reflecting Lu Xun's critical views of the Chinese national character during the late nineteenth and early twentieth centuries. Ah Q bumbles his way through the revolution of 1911 (which brought about the fall of China's last dynasty), but his obsession with petty and

The lone screaming figure in the top panel of Paul Takeuchi's 1996 work *Untitled #13 from Visual Haiku Series* echoes an anxiety that is penned up deep within Ah Q, the protagonist of Lu Xun's 1921 short story "The True Story of Ah Q." An ignorant farm laborer, Ah Q experiences a humiliating series of setbacks, disasters beyond his control, which culminate in his eventually being sent to prison and executed. Ah Q is portrayed as a hapless everyman who typifies the flaws in the modern Chinese national character. Weak willed, he prefers to color his disappointment as petty "spiritual victories" and grasp at insignificant, and often invented, triumphs, somewhat like a hand desperately grasping at lose straws. In the chaos of a revolutionary world, an ability to effectively handle change eludes him. Eventually he is overwhelmed and destroyed by it.

inconsequential issues of personal pride blinds him to the broader social and historical implications of what is going on around him.

The Plot. Ah Q is a rather ordinary peasant living around the time of the fall of the Qing dynasty, in 1911. The first half of the story consists mainly of a series of anecdotes that help sketch out Ah Q's various character defects, focusing in particular on his narrow-mindedness and self-delusion. Constantly mocked and humiliated by his fellow townspeople, Ah Q nevertheless always finds a way to rationalize his situation. He ends up getting involved with the revolutionary movement that helped bring down the Qing dynasty, though he ultimately remains ignorant of its actual political implications. At the end of the story, Ah Q is sentenced as a common thief and executed.

Analysis. "The True Story of Ah Q" takes place against the backdrop of the fall of the Qing dynasty. Ah Q, not fully understanding the political or historical import of this event, decides that it is fashionable to be a revolutionary and therefore eagerly volunteers his services. Satirically, Lu Xun goes on to note that, after the fall of the Qing, many of the same local leaders remain in authority, only now they wear different hats.

Ah Q is a kind of Chinese everyman. In fact, the narrator is not even sure which Chinese ideograph corresponds to the spoken pronunciation of Ah Q's surname. Thus, the "Q" stands for the first letter of the name. Lu Xun's choice of *Q* (it would have been *G* or *K* using modern romanization systems) is particularly effective because it suggests an image of a human head with the braid, or "queue," that all Chinese men were required to wear during the rule of the Manchu-descended Qing dynasty (1644–1911).

Ah Q has come to be one of the most recognizable character types in modern Chinese literature: a rather pathetic figure who consistently rationalizes his own failures by converting them into apparent victories. When Ah Q is asked to sign his execution papers at the end of the story, he has to draw a circle because he does not know how to write his own name. Rather than be humiliated, however, Ah Q imagines he is showing up his executioners by drawing the most perfectly round circle that they have ever seen.

SOURCES FOR FURTHER STUDY

Huang, Martin Weizong. "The Inescapable Predicament: The Narrator and His Discourse in 'The True Story of Ah Q.'" *Modern China* 16, no. 4 (October 1990): 430–449.

"NEW YEAR'S SACRIFICE"

Genre: Short story
Subgenre: Social critique
Published: 1924
Time period: Early twentieth century
Setting: Unspecified

Themes and Issues. Explicitly concerned with issues of the status of women in Chinese society, "New Year's Sacrifice" details the way in which the female protagonist is victimized by her own family, by her in-laws, and finally, by society as a whole. Even the narrative voice of the story (as distinct from Lu Xun's authorial voice) appears to be unwilling or unable to fully appreciate the implications of the protagonist's plight.

The Plot. Like "Diary of a Madman," this story is recounted retrospectively. It opens following the death of the protagonist, identified only as Xianglin's wife. The narrator tries to piece together everything he knows about her life. First, her parents married her to a young boy, and the young woman's in-laws exploited her labor while their son was growing up. The boy, however, died, and she was sent to work as a servant in the narrator's household. Then one day her mother-in-law came to retrieve her and forced her to remarry against her will. After her second husband dies suddenly from typhoid fever and her son is eaten by wolves, Xianglin's wife returns to the narrator's household, a mere shadow of her former self.

After her return Xianglin's wife becomes obsessed with the death of her son and tells anyone who will listen how her son was killed by a wolf who had come down from the mountains; she repeats the story verbatim over and over again. At first, the family members treat her as an oddity and listen out of a sense of curiosity and amusement. Soon, however, they grow tired of both her and her story and come to view her as a source of bad luck.

Analysis. "New Year's Sacrifice" stands as one of Lu Xun's most trenchant critiques of the status of women in traditional Chinese society. Xianglin's wife is doubly stigmatized, first, by the efforts by her family and, later, her in-laws to control who she marries and, second, by the way she is subsequently viewed as a pollutive presence by her former in-laws.

A striking aspect of the story is the way it draws attention to Xianglin's wife's condition by effectively erasing her own voice and then making this very process of erasure a thematic element. As she constantly repeats the story of how her son was eaten by the wolf, she is initially listened to out of a sense of amusement but is soon ignored altogether.

SOURCES FOR FURTHER STUDY

Huters, Theodore. "The Stories of Lu Xun." In *Masterworks of Asian Literature in Comparative Perspective: A Guide for Teaching,* edited by Barbara Stoler Miller. Armonk, NY: Sharpe, 1994, pp. 309–320.

Lu Xun's short story "New Year's Sacrifice" touches on the precarious situation of women in Chinese society. The protagonist is unnamed, referred to only as Xianglin's wife. She asks a scholar who is returning to her town, "After a person dies, does he turn into a ghost or not?" A living ghost herself, by the next day she is dead, finally able to test her theories of the afterlife. For the reader, she has more of a presence in death than in life. Only after her demise do the details of her story emerge. This muted presence is a fate that threatens the young girl in Charles Barbier's ink and prismacolor on paper *Father and Daughter*.

Other Works

"KONG YIJI" (1919). In this, another of Lu Xun's most famous stories, the protagonist, Kong Yiji, is a failed scholar who is now desperately poor. He nevertheless continues to envision himself as a privileged member of society and frequents the local wineshop, where he silently endures the derision of the proprietor and the other customers. The only person who treats him with a modicum of respect is the 12-year-old narrator. By the end of the story, Kong Yiji has had both of his legs broken after he tries to steal from a local scholar. Dragging himself through the mud on his hands, he visits the wineshop one last time. He never shows up again, and everyone presumes that he has finally died.

Like "The True Story of Ah Q," this story is a scathing critique of what Lu Xun perceives to be faults in the Chinese national character. He is critical not only of the heartless cruelty of the customers but also of Kong Yiji's own pathetic pretentiousness. Kong's surname suggests that he is possibly a descendant of Confucius (Kongzi, in Chinese); his treatment in the story signifies the increasing irrelevance of these forms of archaic knowledge to the contemporary world.

WILD GRASS (1927). In addition to his short stories, Lu Xun also wrote *Wild Grass*, a volume of prose poems, which he published in 1926. Although initially not considered one of his better works, many scholars now hold this collection in high regard. Written in a combination of classical Chinese and the modern *baihua* vernacular, it is thought to represent many of the inner contradictions in Lu Xun's personality.

Lu Xun once referred to these prose poems as "small and pale flowers" that bloom "on the rim of hell." The pieces are dark and melancholic, frequently revolving around themes of death, ghosts, and solitude. Their contents often explore the boundaries between dreams and nightmares. One poem, "After Death," opens with the poet dreaming of his own death. In "The Shadow's Farewell" a shadow articulates the way in which its very existence is balanced precariously between the twin abysses of light and darkness, both of which have the power to destroy it.

This collection also contains Lu Xun's only drama, "The Passerby." Written in one act, this piece features a solitary traveler who is trying to decide which road to take. He encounters an old man and a young girl, who appear to represent the older and younger generations in Lu Xun's own China.

OLD STORIES RETOLD (1924). The short pieces in *Old Stories Retold* constitute retellings of classical tales. Lu Xun was clearly attempting to use these retellings to comment on contemporary social conditions, though at times the precise import of this commentary is somewhat vague.

Artistically speaking, the collection is rather uneven, and Lu Xun himself subsequently admitted that he considered it something of a failure. Nevertheless, the project as a whole is conceptually ambitious, and several of the individual pieces are quite memorable.

One of the most engaging and best known of these tales is "Forging the Swords," which presents an interesting twist on an otherwise conventional tale of revenge. The father of the protagonist of the story forges a nearly perfect sword for the king and is then executed so that he will not be able to assist any of the king's enemies in a similar way. Unbeknownst to the king, however, the boy's father had secretly forged a second sword at the same time, which his wife ultimately passes on to their son when he comes of age with the instruction that he avenge the murder of his father.

The son accepts this responsibility and promptly sets out for the capital. On the way he encounters a mysterious man in black, who assures him that his only chance of success will be to allow the stranger first to decapitate him and then to assassinate the king in his place. The story concludes with a rather surreal scene. The stranger succeeds in beheading the king and then throws the heads of both the king and the swordsmith's son, along with his own head, into a large cauldron filled with boiling water, where the heads struggle to bite each other. In the end, the boiling water melts the flesh off each of the heads, and by the time the heads can be retrieved from the cauldron, it has become impossible to differentiate which skull belongs to the king and which to the two assassins. The tale draws attention not only to the workings of revenge but also to the ways in which political power is constructed and imagined.

Resources

"Lu Xun studies" is a minor industry in China and has produced enough publications to fill a small library. Most of those materials, however, are in Chinese, and English-language resources are somewhat more limited.

Lu Xun. Set up by Tim Gallaher, this Web site contains a biographical sketch and links to Lu Xun's works. This chatty and informal site contains a number of useful links to related sites (http://www-hsc.usc.edu/~gallaher/luxun/luxun.html).

Lu Xun Museum in Shanghai. This beautiful and well-funded museum is a useful repository of Lu Xun–related material, as well as an evocative illustration of the degree to which Lu Xun has been lionized in the People's Republic of China. The museum contains various editions of all of his works, a small theater that continuously shows documentaries and movies based on his works, and a life-size mock-up of the last photograph taken of him alive, together with the plaster death mask that a Japanese artist made of his face.

Lu Xun Posters. Part of a larger site on communist propaganda posters, this page contains reproductions of several posters relating to Lu Xun (http://www.iisg.nl/~landsberger/lx.html).

Lu Xun Studies Web Page. Put together by the *Journal of Modern Chinese Literature and Culture,* this is the most complete and up-to-date compilation of primary and secondary material on Lu Xun in English. It also includes numerous direct links to material located on-line (http://deall.ohio-state.edu/denton.2/lxbib.htm).

A Shout from Outside the Iron House, Lu Xun. Volume 2 of the video documentary series *The Giants Within: The Portrait of Chinese Writers* (Taipei, Taiwan: Spring International, 1998), this video (produced in Chinese and dubbed into English) contains important biographical material and many interviews with Lu Xun scholars.

CARLOS ROJAS

J. M. Coetzee

BORN: February 9, 1940, Cape Town, South Africa
IDENTIFICATION: English-language novelist and university professor from South Africa, best known as an allegorist and mythmaker about the postcolonial condition; a two-time winner of the prestigious Booker Prize for literature.

SIGNIFICANCE: Coetzee is one of South Africa's most admired English-language writers; he is known primarily for his novels but also for his memoirs and collections of essays. His novels deal with the predicament of those who endured South African apartheid (legalized racial segregation) and with South Africa's future as a country recovering from a sometimes brutal colonial past. A writer of challenging yet technically brilliant fiction and an outspoken critic of censorship and all forms of political repression, he has won international praise and is acknowledged as one of the most important figures in the field of postcolonial literature.

The Writer's Life

John Michael Coetzee was born in Cape Town, South Africa, on February 9, 1940, and grew up in a remote part of the Cape province known as the Karoo. After starting a career as a college English teacher, Coetzee turned in 1974 to writing fiction. As of 2002 he was living in Cape Town and teaching at its university. He has kept his life so private that many basic facts, such as the names of family members, are not public knowledge.

Childhood. Coetzee's parents were professionals; his father was a lawyer, his mother a schoolteacher. When Coetzee was eight, his father, employed by the government, was fired for his opposition to the official introduction of apartheid. The family moved from Cape Town to Worcester, a small town, where Coetzee's father farmed sheep. Though the family spoke English at home, with relatives Coetzee sometimes conversed in Afrikaans, the South

J. M. Coetzee has come full circle. Receiving his initial academic training at the University of Cape Town, shown here tucked at the base of Table Mountain, the novelist is now the Arderne Chair of Literature at the school. Professor David Lurie, the protagonist of Coetzee's 1999 novel, *Disgrace,* is also an instructor at a Cape Town university. Semiautobiographical in his conception, the character departs from the facts of Coetzee's own life when he is dismissed from his post for misconduct, a move typical of the author's often grim humor.

African Dutch dialect. Coetzee's lineage is partly Afrikaner (Dutch South African), the group most associated in South Africa with antiblack legislation and practices. Both linguistically and politically, the Coetzees occupied a complicated position. White South Africans were in positions of enormous privilege, as the harsh laws of apartheid restricted life for black South Africans. Coetzee, like many keen observers of life in his homeland, was quick to disagree with the unjust arrangements he saw around him and quick to wonder how to reform them.

University Life. Coetzee graduated from the University of Cape Town in 1961, and during a stay in England, he wrote a thesis on the British novelist Ford Madox Ford for a master's degree, awarded by the University of Cape Town in 1963. Coetzee married the same year.

In 1965 Coetzee moved to Austin, Texas, where he wrote his doctoral dissertation, on Samuel Beckett, at the University of Texas. Beckett was a twentieth-century Irish novelist and playwright who explored the tragic aspects of human life by presenting them at their most absurd extremes. Beckett's influence on Coetzee's novels was to be significant. Rather than resort to heavy-handed moralizing about apartheid, as many South African writers had begun to do, Coetzee learned from Beckett to "cleave to the malady." In other words, Coetzee's writing is profoundly sensitive to even the darkest aspects of human life and avoids crude oversimplification.

During his years in Texas, Coetzee was not entirely sure why he was studying English literature. Adrift in the library, he found seventeenth-century records of exploration in southern Africa, including one written by

The aesthetic sensibilities of the novelist and playwright Samuel Beckett (above) closely match those of J. M. Coetzee. Both authors infuse their work with tragicomic elements, imbuing their characters with an underpinning sense of desperation and hopelessness. They each question the monotony of existence and people's responses to life in the face of it.

Jacobus Coetzee, an ancestor. His dissertation was completed in an atmosphere of increasing political upheaval, as the United States escalated its war in Vietnam. Still, Coetzee, who opposed the war, considered his scholarly work in the United States as useful as any other activity and later wrote of this decision, "It was not obvious where one went to escape knowledge [of the war]."

In 1968 Coetzee took a teaching job at the State University of New York at Buffalo, a campus embroiled in the antiwar movement. In Buffalo, Coetzee began work on *Dusklands* (1974), drawing on what he considered two

Coetzee poses for the camera during a publicity shoot, date unknown. J. M. Coetzee's simple and somewhat unadorned prose style belies the layered and richly textured worlds his characters inhabit. His protagonists are marked with a moral complexity that complicates their notions of who they are and their role in the societies they tread. Often the oppressor and the oppressed are portrayed as one and the same. In *Disgrace,* Professor David Lurie is a sexual predator who is forced to face the true implications of his behavior when his daughter is brutally raped by a group of attackers.

HIGHLIGHTS IN COETZEE'S LIFE

1940 John Michael Coetzee is born February 9, in Cape Town, South Africa.

1961 Graduates from University of Cape Town.

1963 Marries.

1964 Completes master's degree at University of Cape Town.

1969 Completes doctorate at the University of Texas, Austin.

1972 Is refused permanent residence in the United States; returns to Cape Town.

1974 First novel, *Dusklands,* appears.

1977 *In the Heart of the Country* is published.

1980 Coetzee wins James Tait Black Memorial Prize and Faber Memorial award; *Waiting for the Barbarians* is published; Coetzee quietly divorces his wife.

1983 Is awarded Booker Prize for *The Life and Times of Michael K.*

1985 Is awarded Prix Fémina (France).

1986 Publishes *Foe.*

1987 Receives Jerusalem Prize for literature (Israel).

1988 Is made a fellow of the Royal Society of Literature, England.

1989 Becomes honorary fellow, Modern Language Association (United States).

1990 Receives Sunday Express Book of the Year award; publishes *Age of Iron.*

1994 Receives Mondello Prize (Italy).

1999 Receives Booker Prize for *Disgrace.*

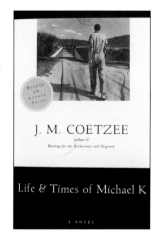

comparable imperialist campaigns: those of the Americans in Vietnam and the Dutch in South Africa. In 1972, refused a green card by American immigration officials, he returned home and accepted a teaching position at the University of Cape Town, where he was professor of general literature as of 2002. During the 1980s and 1990s Coetzee was a visiting professor at several American universities. He has also won many prestigious literary awards and is the first writer to win the Booker Prize on two occasions: in 1983, for *The Life and Times of Michael K,* and again in 1999, for *Disgrace.*

A Man Apart. Coetzee lives a private, almost reclusive, life in a nation where writers face public scrutiny almost incessantly. South African novelists, who faced censorship and political attacks if they commented on the injustice of apartheid, were particularly subject to exposure. Coetzee has never welcomed publicity and avoids autobiographical references in his writing. This deliberate seclusion on his part has ensured that the public details of his life are few, although he has published a fictionalized autobiography, *Boyhood* (1997). Coetzee considers the novelist's proper place the private, inner world of readers, a view of

Maxine Solomon's oil-on-canvas painting *Who Is to Say?* reflects the duality present in the title character of Coetzee's 1983 novel, *The Life and Times of Michael K.* Michael is a faceless everyman, a shadow figure attempting to seize and proclaim his identity. His fate is at once indistinct from that of other black South Africans, while at the same time his struggle universalizes him.

isolation that he often employs in his novels. He and his wife divorced in 1980; he later lost his son in a car accident. Both events have been kept absolutely private.

The "Writerly" Writer. Instead of writing about South African politics in a plainly realistic manner, Coetzee's preference for impersonality, as well as his thorough training in literature, has prompted a vigorously "textual" kind of fiction. That is to say, his novels are often *about* novels; his work draws attention to its own novelistic tricks and devices and draws on other classics of Western literature.

For example, Coetzee's first novel, *Dusklands,* was a strike at colonialism using the text as a weapon. The novel's portrait of the colonial mind is achieved through two parallel modes of writing: a Defense Department analysis of the U.S. involvement in Vietnam and the travel writing of seventeenth-century explorers of the Cape. (Coetzee here uses the writings of his ancestor.) The fixations found in Coetzee's work are all present in this first novel: the examination of the colonizer's mind, the emphasis on understanding the world through literature, and the challenges to the conventions of the novel.

Coetzee seized instantly upon this question of the "writerliness" of fiction—how fiction must finally confess to being a hoax played on readers by an author, sometimes rather flimsily. He has used this idea, strangely enough, to explore the most vicious of political realities. He followed *Dusklands* with *In the Heart of the Country* (1977), which, like the first novel, is concerned with the traps set by various kinds of writing. In *Waiting for the Barbarians* (1980), Coetzee shifts to the form of a moral parable: the novel tells the story of a man of conscience standing up to the horrors of imperialism, which, he discovers, are also to be found within himself.

Two of Coetzee's novels from the 1980s reflect his interest in the "problem" of the novel's form. With the appearance of *The Life and Times of Michael K* in 1983, Coetzee created the tale of a simple man pursuing his own survival during an imaginary South African civil war, and he inserted into it a novel of ideas.

Inspired by some of the more audacious notions of European philosophy, which declared that meaning, finally, could never be settled definitely, the novel explores the chances of its ever possibly having meaning, even as the story advances. Coetzee's next novel, *Foe* (1986), deals directly with the theme of a classic English novel, Daniel Defoe's *Robinson Crusoe* (1719). In Defoe's story, a white Englishman, washed up on a desert island, establishes a kind of impromptu "colony" and enslaves a native named Friday. In Coetzee's revision of the story, the author tries to let Friday tell the story (even though Friday's tongue has been cut out), and the novel explores the basic neurosis of being the colonizer, or "foe." The novel was an immediate success with readers.

In the 1990s both *Age of Iron* (1990) and *The Master of Petersburg* (1994) took new directions. *Age of Iron* offers a brooding but realistic story about antiapartheid violence in Cape Town, and *The Master of Petersburg* examines the mind of the Russian novelist Fyodor Dostoyevsky. In 1999, when Coetzee was awarded the Booker Prize a second time, for *Disgrace,* many readers encountered a novel that is perhaps less typical of Coetzee. The prose is looser, and the forceful allegories and allusions of earlier works are not in evidence. In exploring the violence of the new South Africa, Coetzee sets the issues within an exploration of animal rights, the result being a comparative study of suffering and cruelty.

A question sometimes raised by Coetzee's critics is whether or not it is possible to engage simultaneously with sophisticated literary questions and also with social issues. Coetzee does not offer readers the "gritty," or realistic, version of history and politics that is commonplace in South African fiction. It is precisely by refusing to go along with the commonplace that Coetzee marks out unique territory. Just as he defies the conventions of the South African apartheid novel, he is defying other forms of orthodoxy—such as the ones that brought South Africa to the breaking point in the first place.

An unexpected influence on Coetzee's novels, among many in the vast canon of European philosophy and literature, is the work of the German philosopher G. W. F. Hegel. From this esoteric source Coetzee acquired a way of thinking about the relationship between the colonizer and the colonized. For Hegel the basic problem of human life was knowing oneself, which depends upon knowing the difference between one's own consciousness and that of others. Hegel's classic example of this "knowing" is that of the master and the slave.

The master has power over the slave; the slave is subject to the master. The arrangement seems stable, but it is not. Rather than simply crush the will of the slave, the master must encourage him to work, and in working, the slave transforms his mere subservience into mastery over his environment. Hegel declares that this mastery allows the slave some measure of self-realization. Meanwhile, for his own self-realization, the master is still entirely dependent on the slave's obedience. Therefore, the two players in this scenario are not simply in a relationship of strength over weakness; they both have strengths and weaknesses, and they assist each other in the campaign for self-knowledge.

Coetzee's use of this paradigm, in which a relationship that seems one sided becomes far more complex, is evident in several of his novels and indeed seems ready-made for narrating stories about South African apartheid. *Waiting for the Barbarians* offers a story about a colonial magistrate who profoundly misunderstands his own blame in the violence of imperial conquest. When "barbarians" increase their defiance of the state, the empire responds with extreme brutality. Then the barbarians lead imperial troops out to the desert and simply disappear. With no barbarians, how can the empire define itself? With no slaves, who are the masters? The title of the novel suggests the suspense of colonial interdependence: the magistrate is not simply waiting in fear, he is actually waiting in anticipation.

Language, particularly the language of oppression, factors heavily in the writings of Coetzee. This sign presents its message of restriction in English and Afrikaans, languages foreign to and imposed on its intended nonwhite audience.

The Writer's Work

Coetzee's fiction resides expressly in the historical moment and literary development known as postcolonialism. He has taken on several of the challenges offered by postcolonial perspectives and has overhauled them for his own purposes. The result is difficult to categorize and often painful to read but sometimes extraordinarily powerful.

Postcolonial Themes. The twentieth century saw the large-scale end of colonial rule by European powers over their dependent states in Africa and Asia. With the emergence of new nations came the emergence of new literary voices, chiefly those that had been silent during colonial rule. Among newly independent African nations, for instance, Nigeria became especially prolific in literary output: the Nigerian writers Wole Soyinka, Chinua Achebe, and Ken Saro-Wiwa became spokespeople for the wonder and infamy of Nigerian postcolonial life. In South Africa, however, colonial rule not only persisted but also became ever more repressive under a system known as apartheid, the Afrikaans word for "apartness." Coetzee, who had read widely in postcolonial fiction in graduate school, began writing in the 1970s, as the apartheid system became the acknowledged scandal of the world.

The characteristics of postcolonial fiction are wide ranging, but they tend to cohere around heated denunciations of the former colonizer, including its language, culture, laws, and institutions. For example, in V. S. Naipaul's novel *A Bend in the River,* which is about a revolution in a fictional African country, the former colonial subjects destroy any vestige of British rule, even down to the bronze plaques of English writing affixed to the sides of buildings. The postcolonial novel has a recurring theme of sudden and lurid violence, usually of a former subject against the master or sometimes of a

Misha Gordin's 1986 artwork *Shout #16* presents the moral and social blindness on which much of Coetzee's work hinges. In order to establish and ensure a regime of power, officials and citizens alike needed to remain willfully aloof to the atrocities and oppressive policies of South Africa's government.

colonist torturing a native. Coetzee has made use of this motif in several of his novels, such as *Dusklands, Waiting for the Barbarians,* and *Disgrace.* Coetzee has written elsewhere about the lure of violence in writing about South Africa: In a nation where it was illegal even to photograph prisons, the imagined scenes of torture behind their walls became the lowest kind of novelistic temptation. Spectacle and vulgarity were the inevitable result. Violence, as described in some South African novels, became state-sponsored entertainment. "The true challenge," declared Coetzee, "is how not to play the game by the rules of the state, how to establish one's own authority, how to imagine torture and death on one's own terms."

Rather than chronicle the settling of an old score, the postcolonial novel, when it is successful, dramatizes the problem of knowing what to do once liberation has come. When one has cast colonialism as purely wicked and its opponents as purely good, the task at hand is clear—but once the war is won, what next?

Postcolonial Identity. Postcolonial fiction, therefore, explores the crisis of identity and knowledge in a world where victory, though welcome, has also produced confusion, disorder, and chaos. The postcolonial subject, quite literally, does not now know who he or she is. How does one "de-colonize" the mind? In Coetzee's novels, typically, the crisis is not presented as a melodrama of bewilderment and disorientation but rather as a series of wonderful and surprising encounters and clashes with European culture, which becomes transformed in a South African setting. In his novel *Foe,* for example, the classic imperial story turns upside down when Friday's voice, inaudible in the original telling of the story by Daniel Defoe, becomes a factor in the plot. Coetzee's Friday is mute, and the possibilities of his telling a story are tangled up in his finding an individual voice.

Postcolonial fiction has a final attribute: a preoccupation with the ways language is used. The English language was introduced to South Africa (along with Dutch) by conquerors; it was the colonial medium. Drawing on the work of the French theorist Michel Foucault, many postcolonial thinkers have pointed out that language is not a neutral instrument to convey information; rather, it reflects the power of the speaker or writer. In other words, what one knows or can know depends on a person's relationship to authority. In colonial Africa such issues were more than theoretical: knowing the correct language and how to use it could mean the difference between poverty and wealth or imprisonment and freedom or life and death.

For postcolonial novelists this question of the power of language is fundamental. Concerns over language come up, for example, in the emphasis on dialects and patois, or "street talk," that appear in this type of fiction. Coetzee has taken this issue of literary voices a step further and regularly combines a startling variety of text forms in one novel: European classics, South African lore, colonial administrative documents, inner monologues, police reports, overheard conversations, gossip, and all kinds and levels of language. Even when he narrates scenes of extreme violence, as in *Waiting for the Barbarians,* he is attentive to the ways that language shapes the mind, not the other way around.

BIBLIOGRAPHY

Ashcroft, Bill, Gareth Griffiths, and Helen Tiffin. *The Empire Writes Back: Theory and Practice in Post-Colonial Literatures.* London: Routledge, 1989.

Bhabha, Homi K., ed. *Nation and Narration.* New York: Routledge and Kegan Paul, 1990.

Booker, M. Keith, ed. *The African Novel in English: An Introduction.* Oxford, UK: James Currey, 1998.

Gurnah, Abdulzarak, ed. *Essays on African Writing.* Vol. 1, *A Re-evaluation.* Oxford, UK: Heinemann Educational, 1993.

— *Essays on African Writing.* Vol. 2, *Contemporary Literature.* Oxford, UK: Heinemann Educational, 1995.

Owomoyela, Oyekan, ed. *A History of Twentieth-Century African Literatures.* Lincoln: University of Nebraska Press, 1993.

Wright, Derek, ed. *Contemporary African Fiction.* London: Pluto, 1998.

THE LIFE AND TIMES OF MICHAEL K

Genre: Novel
Subgenre: Parable
Published: 1983
Time period: Late twentieth century
Setting: South Africa

Themes and Issues. This extraordinary novel won the Booker Prize and South Africa's CNA Prize when it appeared in 1983. In the tale of Michael K, Coetzee has created a story of death and decorum, borrowing from adventure novels, surrealist fiction, and Greek tragedy along the way. Although no races are explicitly mentioned and hardly any place-names are offered, the landscape is clearly South African and the setting is that of apartheid. The novel offers what Michael K is seeking all along: a self beyond his official state identity and a destiny greater than his unknown last name.

The Plot. In South Africa civil administration is collapsing under the pressure of years of civil strife. An obscure young gardener named Michael K sets out to take his ailing mother back to her rural home. Michael K does not know his father, and his deformity, a harelip, had prevented him as an infant from suckling at his

The interplay of freedom and containment and the regulation of movement are central concerns in *The Life and Times of Michael K.* Here, children gather near a border they are not allowed to cross. Apartheid fundamentally empties Michael of hope and dignity and numbs him to the extent that imprisonment and death become options that he willingly seeks.

NONFICTION

1986   A Land Apart: A South African Reader (coedited with André Brink)
1988   White Writing: On the Culture of Letters in South Africa
1992   Doubling the Point: Essays and Interviews
1996   Giving Offense: Essays on Censorship
1999   The Lives of Animals

MEMOIRS

1997   Boyhood: Scenes from Provincial Life

NOVELS

1974   Dusklands
1977   In the Heart of the Country
1980   Waiting for the Barbarians
1983   The Life and Times of Michael K
1986   Foe
1990   Age of Iron
1994   Master of Petersburg
1999   Disgrace

TRANSLATIONS (FROM AFRIKAANS)

1975   A Posthumous Confession (by Marcellus Emants)

1984   The Expedition to the Baobab Tree (by Wilma Stockenstrom)

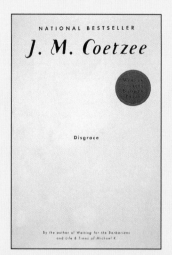

mother's breast. However, he wishes to let his mother end her days in a place where she once was happy, if only he could travel there. The pass laws, South Africa's permit requirements for blacks who wish to travel, force him to go by stealth. On the way, Michael K's mother dies, and he is left alone in an anarchic world of roaming guerrillas. For a time he lives alone on the plot of ground where he buried his mother, a castaway who finally breathes free. He makes things grow. Alone, he begins to experience individuality.

However, civilization catches up with Michael K. A civil war has begun, and he is found by a guerrilla army and taken prisoner. In a prison camp Michael K, the grower of food, starves himself. Once briefly his own man, he is now unable to bear confinement and escapes, determined to live with dignity. He returns to Cape Town. "I was mute and stupid in the beginning," he reflects, "I will be mute and stupid in the end."

Analysis. Michael K's name echoes that of Joseph K., the creation of the German novelist Franz Kafka. Joseph K. was the consummate victim of tyranny in Kafka's novel *The Trial.* Coetzee has created a similar victim of state violence and despotism. Coetzee's novel is bleak and demanding, and its pace and violence are unrelenting. His purpose in creating such a miserable world, of war and brutality and loss, is not to shock readers into awareness of the horrors of apartheid (although many will be shocked) but rather to explore the tests of endurance built into the human experience in general and the partial victory of one nearly anonymous man over them all. At the novel's end, Michael K recedes into the background instead of triumphing explicitly over the many forms of wickedness in his world. He is chiefly capable of survival: in Coetzee's view, this alone is an extraordinary achievement.

SOURCES FOR FURTHER STUDY

Hawthorne, Mark D. "A Storyteller without Words: J. M. Coetzee's *Life and Times of Michael K.*" *Commonwealth Novel in English* 6, nos. 1-2 (Spring 1993): 121-132.

Joffe, P. "The Naming of Michael K: J. M. Coetzee's *Life and Times of Michael K.*" *Nomina Africana* 4, no. 1 (Apr. 1990): 89–98.

Coetzee's 1986 novel, *Foe,* references a longstanding literary tradition in turning to *Robinson Crusoe* for its inspiration. Crusoe and Friday, the fictional characters created by author Daniel Defoe, are seen here rescuing a Spaniard in an illustration that accompanied the legendary novel. Coetzee finds a correlative for contemporary South Africa in Defoe's 1719 novel in which adventure is tempered with concerns of colonialism and enslavement. Who will speak for the Fridays of the world, Coetzee argues, when the enslaved are divested of their tongues, their own life stories?

Moses, Michael Valdez. "Solitary Walkers: Rousseau and Coetzee's *Life and Times of Michael K.*" *South Atlantic Quarterly* 93, no. 1 (Winter 1994): 131–156.

Wittenberg, Hermann. "Michael K and the Rhetorics of Walking." *Inter Action* 4 (1996): 35–37.

Wright, Derek. "Black Earth, White Myth: Coetzee's Michael K." *Modern Fiction Studies* 38, no. 2 (Summer 1992): 435–444.

FOE

Genre: Novel
Subgenre: Metafiction
Published: 1986
Time period: Eighteenth century
Setting: South Africa

Themes and Issues. In this luminous revision of Daniel Defoe's classic tale *Robinson Crusoe* (1719), Coetzee explores the relationships between speech and silence, master and slave, story and storyteller, and sanity and madness. Considered the most "colonial" of English novels, *Robinson Crusoe* is also a ripe candidate for one of Coetzee's favorite themes, namely exploration—both of new territory and of the mind of the colonizer.

The Plot. The novel is at first a sea adventure: Susan Barton, searching for her kidnapped child in the New World, finds herself marooned on an island in the Atlantic with an Englishman named Robinson Cruso and his mute (that is, mutilated) slave, Friday. Cruso is not the enterprising colonizer of Defoe's version, eager to return to England; instead, he is content with his miniature realm and has largely given up on the world. Rescued after a year of Cruso's company and back in England with Friday in tow (Cruso dies on the voyage back, heartsick for his island), Susan Barton approaches the author Daniel Foe and offers him the story. Foe is bored by the idea until Susan suggests that Friday tell the story. Friday's tongue was cut out by persons unknown, but Susan is confident that she can speak for him. Foe, for his part, thinks Friday could simply learn to write. The book is never published. Susan recovers her lost child.

Analysis. This novel is one of Coetzee's most metafictional, that is, it is concerned with a source text (*Robinson Crusoe*) and with drawing attention to its own construction and provisionality. It is also a kind of manifesto about the kinds of liberties a novel can take with its readers: evidently, anything goes. The story that Susan attempts to sell for profit takes several forms along the way—it is Susan's story, it is Foe's, it is Cruso's, it is partly Friday's, and they all share the spotlight with Coetzee and Defoe. Coetzee indifferently moves the author's "authority" from person to person, never declaring in the end which authority is the final one.

To take an old story, some 250 years old, and retell it afresh represents Coetzee's most audacious and yet most typical fictional gesture. His notion of the past, as the past was told in Defoe's 1719 novel, is elastic and changeable: it may be molded to suit new occasions. Coetzee imagines that past in a modified state, one that is more forthcoming about its own colonial burdens. *Foe* acknowledges not only the political realities behind exploration in the New World but also the ways that the very form of the novel, which was Defoe's particular expertise, props up that imperial worldview.

SOURCES FOR FURTHER STUDY

Dragunoiu, Dana. "Existential Doubt and Political Responsibility in J. M. Coetzee's *Foe.*" *Critique* 42, no. 3 (Spring 2001): 309–326.

Gauthier, Marni. "The Intersection of the Postmodern and the Postcolonial in J. M. Coetzee's *Foe.*" *English Language Notes* 34, no. 4 (June 1997): 52–71.

Hardin, Michael. "Colonizing the Characters of Daniel Defoe: J. M. Coetzee's *Foe.*" *Notes on Contemporary Literature* 31, no. 5 (2001): 9–10.

WAITING FOR THE BARBARIANS

Genre: Novel
Subgenre: Realism
Published: 1980
Time period: Late twentieth century
Setting: A fictionalized South Africa

Themes and Issues. A story of one man's experience of political expedience and brutality,

Africans portage their human cargo out on a hunting excursion. Coetzee's *Waiting for the Barbarians* takes a sharp view of the colonial mind-set and the European powers that built their mighty empires on the backs of the native residents.

set in an unidentified African colony, the novel explores who is really the master and who the slave. The colonial empire is finally the subject of those whom it thinks it rules. The nameless Magistrate stands in for every minor colonial official, baffled by the scale of the imperial enterprise and, when he sees it up close, also disgusted by it.

The Plot. The Magistrate (he is never named) has peacefully run the affairs of a tiny frontier settlement for decades, ignoring the war supposedly coming between the barbarians and the Empire. He considers himself a benevolent ruler and wishes above all to avoid trouble. The home office of the Empire sends out Colonel Joll, who has come to crush the insurgent barbarians. Joll's Third Bureau of secret police, which is based on special law-enforce-

ment units that existed in South Africa, regularly tortures prisoners. The Magistrate is disturbed by this escalation of violence. He is uncritical of the Empire itself but wants to distance himself from its new methods of interrogation.

One of Colonel Joll's victims is a young woman, impassive and broken by her ordeal. The Magistrate takes her in and, between sessions of sex, tends her wounds. Stirred by new sympathies, he decides to return the woman to her tribe, and they journey across a dreary and harsh landscape.

Back home, the Magistrate is charged with treason. He becomes Colonel Joll's next torture victim. Meanwhile, Colonel Joll's troops have marched out to meet the foe, but the barbarians do not engage them in combat; instead, they lure the troops to the farthest reaches of the desert and then leave them. The puzzled Empire retreats. The Magistrate resumes his old duties. The novel ends in the suspense of waiting.

Analysis. Colonel Joll remarks at one point to the Magistrate, "pain is truth." He justifies his torture sessions with this statement, claiming that there is a real plot to be found, masterminded by the prisoners he interrogates. His comment might have been reversed to "truth is pain:" the Magistrate discovers as much, as he observes the collapse of his illusions.

The political point of this novel is that the Empire has made a false enemy of the barbarians, simply in order to continue its life as an empire. The barbarians are not in revolt; the Empire is straightforwardly an aggressor. However, empires require barbarians to keep down. The Magistrate finally grasps this basic fact of human life and goes from ignorance to knowledge; the barbarian, he finds, is really within himself, a result of his complicity.

SOURCES FOR FURTHER STUDY

Bruce, Alastair. "Colonialism and Temporality in *Waiting for the Barbarians*." *Inter Action* 4 (1996): 121–126.

Gallagher, Susan Van Zanten. "Torture and the Novel: J. M. Coetzee's *Waiting for the Barbarians*." *Contemporary Literature* 29, no. 2 (Summer 1988): 277–285.

Moses, Michael Valdez. "The Mark of Empire: Writing, History, and Torture in Coetzee's *Waiting for the Barbarians*." *Kenyon Review* 15, no. 1 (Winter 1993): 115–127.

Wenzel, Jennifer. "Keys to the Labyrinth: Writing, Torture, and Coetzee's Barbarian Girl." *Tulsa Studies in Women's Literature* 15, no. 1 (Spring 1996): 61–71.

DISGRACE

Genre: Novel
Subgenre: Realism
Published: 1999
Time period: 1990s
Setting: South Africa

Themes and Issues. Awarded the Booker Prize (as of 2002, Coetzee was the only writer ever to win it twice), *Disgrace* explores the downfall of one man and presents with haunting and at times intolerable intensity the plight of a country caught in the chaotic aftermath of centuries of racial oppression. The novel offers a horrifying account of the sins of the father being visited on the child. It also suggests that even after political change for the better, human suffering and wickedness go on, unchanged and unchangeable.

The Plot. Set in postapartheid South Africa, *Disgrace* tells of David Lurie, a twice-divorced 52-year-old professor of communications at Cape Technical University. Lurie has created a comfortable, if mechanical and passionless, life for himself. He lives within his means. He fancies himself an expert on the English poet Byron, whose legendary roguishness he admires from a safe historical distance. He wants to write an opera about Byron's adventures in Italy. In short, he considers himself happy. Then he becomes involved with one of his students, and his life falls apart.

Lurie pursues his relationship with the young Melanie obsessively and narcissistically. He rapes her. When Melanie and her father press charges, Lurie faces an academic committee, where he admits his guilt but refuses to express any repentance for his acts. The scandal ruins his life, his reputation, his work, and his safety. He is forced to resign and flees to his daughter Lucy's country house. There he struggles to make peace with Lucy and to understand the changing relations of blacks and whites in the new South Africa, such as those of Lucy and her neighbor Petrus, a black entrepreneur. When three black strangers appear at Lucy's house asking to use the telephone, they beat and partly blind Lurie and rape his daughter. Back in Cape Town, Lurie discovers his home has been vandalized, and he decides to stay on with his daughter, who is pregnant with the child of one of her attackers. He begins work on the Byron opera, and in his disarranged mind, it bizarrely includes a scene with a composition for the banjo. Utterly humiliated, Lurie volunteers at the animal clinic,

As in this period illustration of an attack on a group of colonists, the suppressed rage of three black South Africans can find no other outlet but in a burst of violence in the 1999 novel *Disgrace*. When he is beaten and his daughter is raped, David Lurie is forced to make some bitter realizations about the historical legacy he and his nation have inherited. "He speaks Italian, he speaks French, but Italian and French will not save him here in darkest Africa. He is helpless . . . a missionary . . . waiting with clasped hands and upcast eyes while the savages jaw away in their own lingo preparatory to plunging him into their boiling cauldron. Mission work: what has it left behind, that huge enterprise of upliftment? Nothing that he can see."

where he helps destroy the diseased and unwanted dogs—lost, ruined animals like himself.

Analysis. *Disgrace* offers an escalating series of humiliations and devastations to its main character and ends with Lurie incinerating dead dogs. Lurie is basically unregenerate throughout the story and is soundly punished only because, mores having changed, university campuses now penalize sexual predation by their faculty members.

Since apartheid ended, South Africa has had a skyrocketing rate of violent crime. It is uncertain, though, whether Lurie's sufferings are grand and meaningful, whether they stand for the unpunished crimes of all South African whites against blacks. He is, in part, simply a random victim of change, but his fate also suggests that his comfortable life, propped up by apartheid, must be answered for. Lurie's unrepentance only clinches the tragedy: he believes himself to be an innocent man, without obligations to others. Even his work disposing of dogs is done offhandedly, not out of a deep devotion to animals. Coetzee offers a portrait of an unlikable man, one perhaps all too representative of modern South Africa.

SOURCES FOR FURTHER STUDY

Attridge, Derek. "Age of Bronze, State of Grace: Music and Dogs in Coetzee's *Disgrace*." *Novel* 34, no. 1 (Fall 2001): 98–121.

Gorra, Michael. "After the Fall." *New York Times*, November 28, 1999.

Lehmann-Haupt, Christopher. "Caught in Shifting Values (and Plot)." *New York Times*, November 11, 1999.

Maris, Michael. "Very Morbid Phenomena: 'Liberal Funk,' the 'Lucy-Syndrome,' and J. M. Coetzee's *Disgrace*." *Unisa English Studies* 6, no. 1 (2001): 32–38.

Seidel, Linda. "Death and Transformation in J. M. Coetzee's *Disgrace*." *Journal of Colonialism and Colonial History* 2, no. 2 (Winter 2001): 22.

Other Works

BOYHOOD: SCENES FROM PROVINCIAL LIFE (1997). *Boyhood* is the closest Coetzee has come to introducing any part of his own life into his work. It is either a loosely autobiographical novel or a fictionalized autobiography of someone who very much resembles Coetzee (the author refers to his protagonist only as "he"). When his publisher asked him, "Is this fiction or memoir?" Coetzee replied, "Do I have to choose?" The work transforms the raw data of childhood into stories of growing up amid South African apartheid and relates the strange experience of coming of age in such a system. *Boyhood* is full of abrupt changes of scene and ends brusquely. Coetzee's point is that such a world—both for a child and for a subject of apartheid—has little built-in shape and probably should be written about without heavy-handed structure or form. To impose form is to indulge in deception.

The plot focuses on Coetzee's unhappy childhood. His family had left Cape Town in 1948 for the provinces, and Coetzee, a bookish boy, was confounded by his new surroundings. His parents were Afrikaners, but through education and class aspiration they "preferred to be English." The small family, trying to rise in the world and stuck in a small town, has its special tensions, especially when Coetzee takes sides with his mother against his father. Imagination should be the young Coetzee's escape, and *Boyhood* offers charming evidence of the writer's youthful literary mind. Asked to choose sides in the global cold war, he favors Russia over the United States simply because he greatly cherishes the letter *R*. Bored by school essay assignments, he also declares at an early age that he will be a writer.

Primarily, *Boyhood* is about the problem of being truthful about one's own life. Coetzee, a skilled critic of literature as well as a novelist, is under no illusions. Memory can often provide more elaborate fiction than the imagination.

GIVING OFFENSE: ESSAYS ON CENSORSHIP (1996). Written during the 1980s and 1990s, *Giving Offense* is an extraordinary collection of Coetzee's articles on the subject of control of the written word by governments—South Africa's in particular. His somewhat unorthodox argument about why censorship is wrong is animated by the fact that Coetzee, unlike many of his readers, had lived in a police state. This firsthand knowledge quickens and sharpens his account.

To understand Coetzee's views and highlight their significance, it is useful to know the arguments against censorship that are frequently offered. Free expression, goes the argument, is an absolute value: ideas and artworks must be allowed to circulate without censorship, even though they are offensive to some people. Even material judged morally offensive deserves legal protection because it may contain politically subversive ideas, which must be allowed free expression. Often, a judgment about an artwork's moral obscenity may be a reaction to the political point of the artwork. Thus, morally offensive material should also enjoy protected status, because of the presumption that it may have a political dimension.

When Coetzee completed *Boyhood,* his publisher asked him, "Is this fiction or memoir?" to which the author replied, "Do I have to choose?" The book defies categorization, employing elements of both fact and fiction. The use of the third person adds the often ironic and comic distance Coetzee needed to scrutinize the choices he made and paths he took as a child.

In South Africa the legal system makes no distinction between morals and politics. Thus, for Coetzee, arguments that relate or contrast the two kinds of censorship are irrelevant and distracting. Freedom of artistic expression must be defended on other grounds.

Coetzee's approach to the issue is quite startling. In the introduction to the collection, Coetzee takes on the controversial question of protecting children from pornographic images. "Children," he argues, "are not innocent"; nor do adults, he goes on, "inherently possess dignity." Both concepts are "foundational fictions." If the innocence of children is not at stake and the dignity of humanity is beside the point, then why bother to regulate pornography? It can do little harm. To puff oneself up as a "dig-nified" and "protective" monitor of what children can see will lead only to greater perversion. This position is typical of Coetzee's paradoxical thinking. His dry-eyed look at children and pornography is consistent with his tendency to look horrors straight in the eye.

Presented in twelve chapters that cover everything from Stalinism in Russia to apartheid in South Africa and feminism in America, *Giving Offense* seeks not to simplify the issue of censorship but to complicate it. Far from being a melodrama of noble defenders of truth against evil state officials, censorship has implications that are subtle and irregular and surprising. Coetzee finds in this political question a consummate example of the serious risk of thinking simply about a complex problem.

Resources

The Internet is rich in opportunities for further research into the life and works of J. M. Coetzee. What follows is merely a sampling.

Booker Prize. England's most prestigious literary award, the Booker Prize, offers on its Web site a large archive of winners' biographies, lists of their works, and facts about the authors who have won it, including J. M. Coetzee (http://www.bookerprize.co.uk).

Coetzee's Biography and Works are also listed at a Web site created by two faculty members at the University of Tennessee. The site offers a lengthy assortment of secondary sources for further reading (http://www.utc.edu/~engldept/booker/coetzee.htm).

The Guardian. This British newspaper has assembled at its Web site a variety of links related to Coetzee. They are well chosen and lively (http://books.guardian.co.uk/authors/author/0,5917,-43,00.html).

New York Times. This newspaper offers a compendium of articles, both by and about Coetzee, that have been reprinted from its book review section (http://www.nytimes.com/books/97/11/02/home/coetzee.html).

Postcolonial Web. This Singapore-based Web site offers a wealth of information on postcolonial theory and literature. Coetzee figures strongly in this literary movement (http://www.scholars.nus.edu.sg/landow/post/index.html).

KRIS FRESONKE

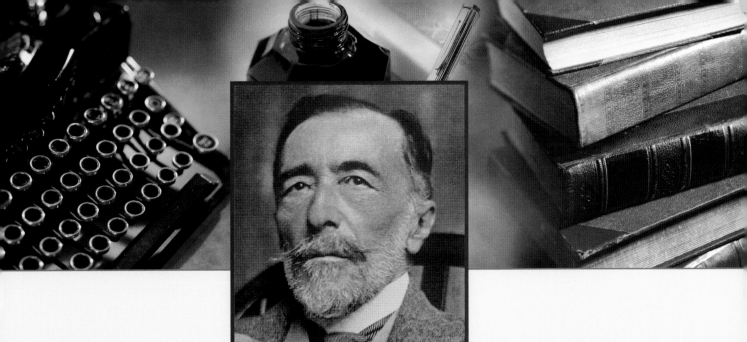

Joseph Conrad

BORN: December 3, 1857, Berdyczów (now Berdichev), Ukraine
DIED: August 3, 1924, Bishopsbourne, England
IDENTIFICATION: Late-nineteenth- and early-twentieth-century British writer best known for his psychological fiction, much of which is set in the maritime world of Southeast Asia.

SIGNIFICANCE: Joseph Conrad's powerful investigations into psychological and moral issues, along with his experimentation with narrative form and his questioning of traditional cultural beliefs, have placed him at the forefront of twentieth-century British literature. He is most appreciated for the fiction he wrote between 1897 and 1912 and continues to be read and studied around the world. His most widely read works, *Heart of Darkness* and *Lord Jim,* exemplify his profound literary significance, as they deal with issues no less important than the nature of Western civilization and indeed of human existence itself.

Józef Teodor Konrad Nałęcz Korzeniowski was born on December 3, 1857, to Apollo Korzeniowski and his wife, Ewelina (Eva) Bobrowska Korzeniowski. Conrad's parents came from the Polish nobility. His father was also a writer of some reputation who worked vigorously for Polish independence from Russia.

Childhood and Youth. As a result of his revolutionary activities, Apollo Korzeniowski's family was exiled, first to Vologda, Russia, and later to Chernikov. Conrad's mother died of tuberculosis in 1865, and in 1869 his father died

of the same disease. Apollo Korzeniowski was given a hero's burial and is still considered a national hero in Poland. Conrad, now orphaned, went to live first with his grandmother and then with his uncle Tadeusz Bobrowski. Bobrowski was a practical-minded man who disapproved of his brother-in-law's revolutionary activities; Bobrowski preferred a more gradual and pragmatic approach to Polish independence. He tried to rein in Conrad's naturally adventurous nature and was a moral and financial support to him for many years. Even after Conrad reached adulthood, his uncle re-

A student at a maritime training station in St. Petersburg, Florida, polishes a figurehead of Conrad on the *Joseph Conrad*, the square rigger named after the noted author of sea tales, in 1940. Although Conrad attended maritime school more than sixty years before this student, the two share a bond that erases the years between them: both aspired to be sailors at a tender age.

mained a touchstone of strength for Conrad until Bobrowski's death in 1894.

Life in France. As a child and youth Conrad was a voracious reader, and although his reading tastes were quite broad, he was particularly fond of adventure fiction. At 17, after two years of importuning his uncle, Conrad convinced Bobrowski to let him pursue a life at sea, and thus Conrad's roughly 20-year maritime life began. He first moved to Marseilles, France, to attend maritime school and work on seagoing vessels, with the ultimate goal of joining the French maritime service. Conrad had studied French as a youth and became fluent in the language. Bobrowski gave Conrad a generous allowance, but Conrad consistently lived beyond his means. It was during this time that one of Conrad's most notorious adventures occurred: he received a bullet wound in the chest. He later claimed that the wound resulted from a duel, but a letter from Bobrowski to a friend suggests that it was actually an attempted suicide.

Life at Sea. Conrad eventually recovered from his wound, and upon discovering that he was ineligible to enter the French maritime service (because he was subject to up to 25 years of Russian military conscription as a result of his father's revolutionary activities), he joined the British merchant fleet (which did not have the same restrictions). During Conrad's life at sea, he traveled to South America, Africa, Southeast Asia, and many other parts of the world. He had various experiences in the maritime trade; he even reputedly smuggled arms. He rose through the ranks, to the positions of second mate, first mate, and eventually master in 1886, the same year he became a naturalized British citizen. In 1888 Conrad obtained his first command, aboard the *Otago*. His experience at sea would eventually serve as the raw material for many of his fictional works. Before joining the British merchant fleet, Conrad knew no English, and although he always spoke with a heavy accent, he came to master the language enough to become one of its finest writers.

Conrad, who forged many literary friendships, poses for a photograph with American writer Ellen Glasgow in England in 1914, (left). Glasgow, whose writing realistically depicted life in her native Virginia, won the Pulitzer Prize in 1942. She was also photographed with Conrad's wife, Jessie (far left); Conrad's older son, Borys (center); and Conrad (far right) in the photograph above.

HIGHLIGHTS IN CONRAD'S LIFE

1857 Józef Teodor Konrad Nałęcz Korzeniowski is born on December 3 in Berdyczów (now Berdichev), Ukraine.

1861 Conrad's father is arrested for activities supporting Polish independence.

1862 Conrad's father and mother are exiled; Conrad accompanies them.

1865 Conrad's mother dies.

1869 Conrad's father dies.

1874 Conrad moves to Marseilles, France, to attend maritime school.

1878 Is wounded, presumably in an attempted suicide; later joins British merchant fleet.

1886 Passes exam to become master; becomes a naturalized British citizen.

1888 Achieves his first command, aboard the *Otago.*

1889 Begins writing *Almayer's Folly.*

1890 Works on a steamboat for a Belgian trading company on the Congo River.

1891 As first mate of the *Torrens,* meets John Galsworthy.

1894 Tadeusz Bobrowski, Conrad's uncle and guardian, dies.

1895 Conrad publishes his first novel, *Almayer's Folly.*

1896 Marries Jesse George.

1897 Meets R. B. Cunninghame Graham, British writer and statesman, and Stephen Crane, American writer.

1898 Conrad's son Borys is born; Conrad meets Ford Madox Ford and H. G. Wells.

1899 *Heart of Darkness* is serialized.

1900 *Lord Jim* is published.

1904 *Nostromo* is published.

1906 Conrad's son John is born.

1907 *The Secret Agent* is published.

1910 "The Secret Sharer" is serialized.

1911 *Under Western Eyes* is published.

1913 *Chance* is published; Conrad finally achieves economic success from his writing.

1914 Revisits Poland.

1917 *The Shadow Line* is published.

1924 Conrad declines knighthood; dies on August 3 and is buried at Canterbury, England.

In 1890 Conrad accepted what would prove to be one of his most important maritime positions, on a steamboat for a Belgian trading company on the Congo River. His experience in the Congo would forever change him; he once remarked, "Before the Congo I was just a mere animal." His Congo experience wreaked havoc on his emotional and physical health, the effects of which stayed with him for the remainder of his life. His Congo command would also become the basis for his most famous work, *Heart of Darkness*. In 1889 Conrad had begun writing what would become his first novel, *Almayer's Folly*. While working on the novel, Conrad continued pursuing his maritime profession. During his time as first mate on the *Torrens*, Conrad met John Galsworthy, a British writer who would become a longtime friend. In 1895 Conrad gave up his life at sea to become a full-time writer and thus entered the final phase of his remarkable life.

Life as a Writer. In 1896 Conrad married Jesse George; she gave birth to their first son, Borys, two years later. Conrad's other son, John, was born in 1906. Conrad's marriage seems to have been generally comfortable and even happy. Conrad was not a particularly easy person with whom to live, given his occasional physical and emotional difficulties and his dark outlook on life, but Jesse was typically an anchor of stability for him, particularly during Conrad's early writing career.

Over the course of the next several years, Conrad made a number of important literary friendships with such authors as Ford Madox Hueffer (better known as Ford Madox Ford), R. B. Cunninghame Graham, Stephen Crane, Henry James, and H. G. Wells. He also became friends with the influential critic Edward Garnett, who would serve as Conrad's literary editor and general supporter throughout the rest of his life. Of these literary friendships the most significant was that with Ford, with whom he collaborated on *The Inheritors, Romance,* and *The Nature of a Crime.*

Although Conrad's first novel, *Almayer's Folly,* received some very favorable reviews, it

FILMS BASED ON CONRAD'S WORKS

1919 *Victory*
1925 *Lord Jim*
1926 *The Silver Treasure* (adapted from *Nostromo*)
1927 *The Road to Romance* (adapted from *Romance*)
1929 *The Rescue*
1930 *Dangerous Paradise* (adapted from *Victory*)
1936 *Sabotage* (adapted from *The Secret Agent*)
1940 *Victory: An Island Tale*
1950 *The Secret Sharer* (TV)
1952 *Outcast of the Islands*
1952 *Face to Face* (adapted from "The Secret Sharer")
1953 *Laughing Anne*
1955 *Heart of Darkness* (TV)
1958 *Heart of Darkness* (TV)
1960 *Victory* (TV)
1965 *Lord Jim*
1967 *The Secret Agent* (TV)
1967 *The Rover* (TV)
1972 *The Secret Sharer* (TV)
1975 *The Secret Agent* (TV)
1975 *Under Western Eyes* (TV)
1976 *The Shadow Line* (TV)
1977 *The Duellists* (adapted from "The Duel")
1979 *Apocalypse Now* (adapted from *Heart of Darkness*)
1981 *An Outpost of Progress*
1992 *The Secret Agent* (TV)
1994 *Heart of Darkness* (TV)
1996 *The Secret Agent*
1997 *Nostromo* (TV)
1997 *Swept from the Sea* (adapted from "Amy Foster")

was not until 1897, with the publication of *The Nigger of the "Narcissus"* and its famous preface, that Conrad's true creative abilities were realized. During roughly the next 15 years he published a remarkable series of novels and tales, all literary masterpieces, among them *Heart of Darkness, Lord Jim,* "Youth," "Typhoon," *Nostromo, The Secret Agent,* "The Secret Sharer," and *Under Western Eyes.*

Despite the critical success, the life of a writer tried Conrad. Writing was for him a difficult and painful process, often leaving him exhausted and even leading to emotional breakdowns, most notably after completing *Under Western Eyes.* Furthermore, the financial returns on Conrad's works did not match the critical returns, and Conrad was chronically short of cash. In addition, continually living beyond his means exacerbated his financial difficulties.

In 1913, with the publication of *Chance,* however, Conrad finally achieved the financial stability that he had so long sought. From then on, he continued to receive ever greater financial success and public acclaim for his writing. Conrad returned to his native Poland in 1914, only to be caught in the outbreak of the First World War; he and his family narrowly escaped and returned to England.

Conrad continued writing until the end of his life. Many believe, though, that except for *The Shadow Line,* Conrad's later work lacks the power and substance of his earlier work. When Conrad died of a heart attack, on August 3, 1924, his novel *Suspense* remained unfinished. He was buried in nearby Canterbury, England, leaving behind a remarkable life and legacy, unmatched except by the very greatest writers in the history of English literature.

Conrad at the door of his home in Kent, in southeastern England, where he wrote the story "Tomorrow," which eventually became his 1920 play, *One Day More.* Conrad's longtime friend John Galsworthy, the English novelist and playwright who won the Nobel Prize for Literature in 1932, wrote the introduction to *Laughing Anne and One Day More,* a volume containing *One Day More* and Conrad's 1923 play, *Laughing Anne.* Galsworthy, who had intentions of specializing in marine law before becoming a writer, met Conrad while traveling around the world.

The Writer's Work

Although Joseph Conrad wrote nonfiction and a few plays, his novels and short stories are his primary contribution to English literature. His fiction concerns the problems of the individual in an indifferent universe and considers the psychological conflicts that arise as individuals try to construct meaning for their existence and try to reconcile their own needs with the expectations society places upon them. Conrad's narrative innovations echo his thematic interests; he experiments with narrative time and voice to produce works whose formal aspects (narrator, chronology, style) are as challenging as the philosophical issues they raise.

Conrad's Universe. Because he began his literary career relatively late in life, one might suppose that Conrad's view of the world would be similar either to that of some late Victorian writers, who often viewed the world with pessimism, or to that of some middle Victorian writers, who often viewed the world with optimism. Conrad, however, posits an indifferent universe, a universe neither hostile to nor welcoming of humanity but instead indifferent to human needs and wants and empty of inherent meaning. In this way Conrad could be considered the first of the modernist writers (most of whom did not begin writing until after the turn of the century). Like other modernists, Conrad could not accept the traditional Judeo-Christian views that human beings are at the center of the universe, that the universe was created by a benevolent and all-powerful being, and that Western civilization was founded upon absolute truths. In contrast, Conrad consistently presented his characters as creatures out of place in the universe, and he consistently ques-

tioned the presumptions of Western civilization concerning its truth and role in the world. Conrad's characters seek to create meaning in their existence, despite the fact that they can no longer rely upon the truths of the past for support.

Conrad's Narrative Techniques. One of Conrad's crucial contributions to literary history is his use of a variety of narrative techniques. In some cases Conrad introduced a new technique to the narrative process; in oth-

Conrad, rarely thought of as the uninvolved passenger, is seated on the deck of the SS *Tuscania* as it arrives in New York on May 1, 1923, a little more than a year before his death. His novel *Rover* was published the same year.

LONG FICTION

1895 Almayer's Folly
1896 An Outcast of the Islands
1897 The Nigger of the "Narcissus"
1899 Heart of Darkness (serialized)
1900 Lord Jim
1901 The Inheritors (with Ford Madox Ford)
1903 Romance (with Ford Madox Ford)
1904 Nostromo
1907 The Secret Agent
1911 Under Western Eyes
1913 Chance
1914 Victory
1917 The Shadow Line
1919 The Arrow of Gold
1920 The Rescue
1923 The Rover
1924 The Nature of a Crime (with Ford Madox Ford)
1925 Suspense (unfinished)
1928 The Sisters (unfinished)

SHORT FICTION COLLECTIONS

1898 Tales of Unrest
1902 Youth
1903 Typhoon
1908 A Set of Six
1912 'Twixt Land and Sea
1914 Within the Tides
1925 Tales of Hearsay

PLAYS

1920 One Day More
1921 The Secret Agent
1923 Laughing Anne

NONFICTION

1906 The Mirror of the Sea
1912 A Personal Record
1921 Notes on Life and Letters
1926 Last Essays
1983 The Collected Letters of Joseph Conrad

ers he took established techniques and put his own stamp upon them.

Before Conrad's time, the traditional narrative method was chronological: a work of fiction started at the beginning, and the events it enclosed unfolded in unbroken order from beginning to end. In contrast, Conrad's narratives, often moving freely between past, present, and future, fracture the traditional chronological method. Although other writers had experimented with narrative structure, employing such techniques as flashbacks, Conrad's sophisticated use of the nonchronological narrative is original, especially as it appears in *Lord Jim, Nostromo, The Secret Agent,* and *Chance.* These narratives are not fixed in past, present, or future; one narrator may relate material from the past while another relates material from the present. By so doing, Conrad shows that in life events typically do not unfold chronologically; rather, a person may stumble upon the middle of a story before learning either its beginning or its end.

Conrad's use of multiple narrators in his works is another contribution to narrative.

Traditional fiction employed a single narrator (occasionally a second, as in the case of a "frame" narration, where one character tells a story to another, who in turn relates it to the reader). Conrad's fiction, however, often uses numerous narrators to reveal different parts of a story. In *Lord Jim,* for example, at least half a dozen different narrators supply the main narrator, Marlow, with material that he then narrates first to a group of listeners and then later to a single member of that group. This expository method allows Conrad to emphasize that information comes from various sources and is influenced by the individual who narrates it. The method also underpins Conrad's view of the uncertainty of truth and knowledge.

Isolation and Solidarity. A common theme that runs through much if not most of Conrad's work is that of isolation and solidarity. Because he saw Western civilization as without an absolute foundation, Conrad consistently presents his characters as isolated, either physically or psychologically, and then consid-

Like the characters in a typical Conrad sea tale, the sailboat in Caspar David Friedrich's oil-on-canvas nineteenth-century painting *Sea-piece by Moonlight* (Museum der Bildenden Kuenste, Leipzig, Germany) is engulfed in the isolation of the open waters. When indifferent to outside influences and negligent of human needs, its course will be charted by the authority of the uncertain wind.

ers how they can make sense of an existence without inherent sense. In much of his sea fiction, his characters are isolated from the external restraints of Western civilization. Conrad wonders how people respond to their circumstances when there is no law or public opinion to influence them. Similarly, in other works ("The Return," "The Lagoon," and "Karain," among others) he considers the psychological isolation of his characters either when they are unable to establish relationships with others or when they destroy those relationships.

Conrad's solution to the physical and psychological isolation he sees in the human world can be found in the idea of solidarity, or community. Since, for Conrad, there is no inherent meaning in the universe and no inherent truth

behind the laws and customs of Western civilization, the only thing that can provide meaning is communion with other human beings, whether in the form of relationships between two people or in the form of communities. Human beings agree upon rules and customs and thereby create meaning for their lives. Furthermore, they rely on one another for protection and help. This concept is perhaps best represented in Conrad's *The Nigger of the "Narcissus,"* in which each member of the ship's crew must rely on every other crew member, or else they all risk drowning during the storm. Such incidents (a similar one occurs in "Typhoon") are metaphors for the human condition in general. In any community physical and psychological safety necessitates mutual re-

Ruprecht von Kaufmann's oil-on-canvas painting *Soulmates* suggests the power found in solidarity and mutual reliance and embodies Conrad's belief that communion, whether between two individuals or among the members of a community, is the only hope for survival and the only chance to experience true meaning.

liance and solidarity—and so Conrad consistently rejects characters who place ideals or material interests above human relationships.

BIBLIOGRAPHY

Daleski, H. M. *Joseph Conrad: The Way of Dispossession.* London: Faber and Faber, 1977.

Gillon, Adam. *Joseph Conrad.* Boston: Twayne, 1982.

Guerard, Albert J. *Conrad the Novelist.* Cambridge, MA: Harvard University Press, 1958.

Hay, Eloise Knapp. *The Political Novels of Joseph Conrad.* Chicago: University of Chicago Press, 1963.

Jones, Susan. *Conrad and Women.* New York: Oxford University Press, 1999.

Karl, Frederick R. *A Reader's Guide to Joseph Conrad.* Rev. ed. New York: Noonday, 1969.

Moore, Gene M., ed. *Conrad on Film.* Cambridge, UK: Cambridge University Press, 1997.

Moser, Thomas. *Joseph Conrad: Achievement and Decline.* Cambridge, MA: Harvard University Press, 1957.

Najder, Zdzis_aw. *Joseph Conrad: A Chronicle.* New Brunswick, NJ: Rutgers University Press, 1983.

Peters, John G. *Conrad and Impressionism.* Cambridge, UK: Cambridge University Press, 2001.

Stape, J. H., ed. *The Cambridge Companion to Joseph Conrad.* Cambridge, UK: Cambridge University Press, 1996.

Watt, Ian. *Conrad in the Nineteenth Century.* Berkeley: University of California Press, 1979.

Watts, C. T. *A Preface to Conrad.* London: Longmans, 1982.

The Nigger of the "Narcissus"

Conrad's literary career began with the publication of *Almayer's Folly. An Outcast of the Islands* followed shortly thereafter. Although these are both good books in their own right and would perhaps be read more often if someone else had written them, they do not fully show Conrad's abilities. Conrad's third book, however, *The Nigger of the "Narcissus,"* much more fully demonstrates his creative genius.

The novel first appeared in 1897 and draws upon Conrad's experience at sea. In this novel he uses the microcosm of the ship's crew and officers to investigate the workings of society, the relationship between the human world and the natural world, and the place of human beings in the universe. Conrad also unveils for the first time in this work one of his most important themes—isolation and solidarity.

The Preface. Late in his writing career, Conrad wrote a series of "author's notes" to his works in preparation for a collected edition, but these notes typically discuss only the biographical origins of his works. Unlike the author's notes, the preface to *The Nigger of the "Narcissus"* is a statement of Conrad's artistic creed. In this preface Conrad outlines his theory of literature more fully than he does anywhere else in his letters or published works. The preface is eminently quotable and shows Conrad's commitment to becoming an artist rather than merely an author.

Although the preface is not a systematic philosophical statement, Conrad does identify several important ideas concerning what makes a book a work of art. First, a work of art "should carry its justification in every line"; confronted with "the hazardous enterprise of living," artists must reach within themselves and draw out those truths they find there, appealing to the readers' senses. Conrad says, "My task which I am trying to achieve is, by the power of the written word, to make you hear, to make you feel—it is, before all, to make you *see!* That—and no more: and it is everything!" Ultimately, Conrad argues for a solidarity between reader and writer, a communal experience that is established through the work of art.

The Plot. The *Narcissus* is ready to set sail from Bombay, India. Mr. Baker, the chief mate, is calling roll when the last crew member, James Wait, finally arrives. Wait is a black man who coughs throughout the story and once at sea claims he is dying. Within a week of the start of the voyage, Wait has gone to his bunk and remains an invalid in a cabin in the deckhouse for the remainder of the trip. The crew members are unsure whether Wait is really ill or just pretending in order to avoid work. They do not know whether to resent or pity him. While rounding the Cape of Good Hope, they encounter a severe storm that nearly sinks the *Narcissus*. The men risk their lives to free Wait, who is trapped in his cabin. The ship ultimately survives the storm. As they near their destination, Wait appears to grow more ill. At that point, though, he claims he is not dying and demands to be allowed to work again. Certain that Wait is dying, the captain refuses and in so doing nearly invites a mutiny. When the ship finally comes in sight of land, Wait dies and is buried at sea. The *Narcissus* finally arrives at port, and the members of the crew go their separate ways.

Analysis. The men on board the *Narcissus* are isolated from the rest of humanity and must establish their own community. Most, if not all, of them are strangers to one another and enter this new world having to find a way to interact effectively with the others aboard. During the voyage the men discover that without mutual cooperation not only can they not interact effectively, they cannot even survive. It takes the efforts of each man during the storm to save the ship as well as their own lives. Without that cooperative effort the ship would certainly have sunk, and all aboard would have drowned.

Conrad uses the ship's community as a microcosm for human existence as a whole. Human beings arriving in this world are strangers to one another and must establish communities, which require mutual cooperation, in order to provide protection for all and effective social interaction. Conrad sees the perilous and uncertain position of the men on the ship as like that of human beings in general. Finding themselves in an indifferent universe, they must create meaning for their existence through their interaction and relationships with others, as well as through the larger communities they construct.

Three characters embody the ideas Conrad investigates in the novel: Donkin, Wait, and Singleton. Donkin is selfish, lazy, dishonest, and cowardly. He is the single greatest threat to the community on board the ship. He consistently shirks responsibilities and thereby endangers his shipmates. Two incidents in particular exemplify this problem. During the storm, when the efforts of everyone are necessary to save the ship, Donkin, thinking only of himself, refuses even to accompany those who go to free Wait from his cabin. Later he tries to incite the crew to mutiny. During the confrontation between the men and the officers, Donkin throws a belaying pin at the captain and then hides in the anonymity of the crowd. The near mutiny could have resulted in the crew's imprisonment once the ship reached shore. Donkin endangers first their lives and then their freedom.

Wait is particularly important because he represents both a *weight* on the crew and one who *waits* for death. Although the rest of the crew members typically sympathize with Wait, even going so far as to risk the anger of the officers in catering to his whims, they are consistently uncomfortable around him. He be-

The human chain of reliance in David Linn's oil-on-panel work *The Ascent* embodies the cooperative effort of the group as a whole in Conrad's third novel, *The Nigger of the "Narcissus."* Commenting on loyalty, which he deemed so necessary for survival and meaning in an indifferent universe, Conrad wrote in the preface to his 1912 work of nonfiction, *A Personal Record,* "Those who read me know my conviction that the world, the temporal world, rests on a few very simple ideas; so simple that they must be as old as the hills. It rests, notably, among others, on the idea of Fidelity."

This drawing of the *Otago,* Conrad's first command, was created by G. F. W. Hope, one of Conrad's old sea friends. Hope drew it from Conrad's own descriptions of the vessel. Conrad often visited the Hope home while he was completing his first novel, *Almayer's Folly,* from which he would often read to Hope and his wife. Fifteen years later he would dedicate *Lord Jim* to them.

comes for them the literal embodiment of death. In fact, when they suggest that Wait is simply faking illness to avoid work, the charge has less to do with any resentment of him than with their wish to ignore the death he represents, a death eventually awaiting them all.

Singleton appears as the most admirable character in the novel. Presented as old and wizened, he speaks little but does his duty with consistency and accomplishment. During the storm he never leaves his post but continues to steer the ship with mute stoicism. Despite the dangers around him, he accepts his role and does his job. Conrad clearly sees Singleton as the model of how one should act in this world, in this universe indifferent to life and death.

At the end of the novel, as the men go their separate ways and their life aboard ship ends, the *Narcissus* appears dead—much as any man does as he dies and leaves this life.

SOURCES FOR FURTHER STUDY

Allen, Jerry. *The Sea Years of Joseph Conrad.* Garden City, NY: Doubleday, 1965.

Berthoud, Jacques. *Joseph Conrad: The Major Phase.* Cambridge, UK: Cambridge University Press, 1978.

Brus, Paul. *Conrad's Early Sea Fiction.* Lewisburg, PA: Bucknell University Press, 1979.

Burgess, C. F. *The Fellowship of the Craft.* Port Washington, NY: Kennikat Press, 1976.

Schwarz, Daniel R. *Conrad: "Almayer's Folly" to "Under Western Eyes."* Ithaca, NY: Cornell University Press, 1980.

HEART OF DARKNESS

Genre: Novella
Subgenre: Bildungsroman
Published: England, 1899 (serial version)
Time period: 1890s
Setting: London, Brussels, and the Congo

Themes and Issues. *Heart of Darkness* looks at questions of good and evil in human beings, the relationship between Europe and Africa, and human fidelity to a code of behavior. Kurtz, who goes into Africa with ideas of civilizing and improving the Africans, ends up raiding villages and allowing himself to be worshiped as a god. Conrad investigates how this transformation takes place. In the process he also questions the role Europe plays in the exploitation of Africa, and he considers how human beings can maintain fidelity to a code of behavior without such external restraints as judicial laws.

The Plot. Charlie Marlow is sitting on the deck of a cruising ship, relating one of his experiences as a seaman to several listeners, one of whom (unnamed) records the telling of the tale. Marlow was out of work and looking for a new position. He gets a position commanding a steamboat for a Belgian trading company in the Belgian Congo and leaves for Africa shortly thereafter. Arriving at the trading company's station on the coast, he finds inefficiency and wastefulness everywhere. His steamboat is inland, and he has to hike for a number of days before arriving at the company's central station on the Congo River. Once there, Marlow discovers that his steamboat has been sunk, and he spends the next several months waiting for his boat to be repaired. He finds at the central station the same inefficiency and wastefulness he found at the company's outer station. Once his steamer is repaired, Marlow begins his trek up the Congo River on a mission to relieve Kurtz, the trader at the company's inner station and a man reputedly idealistic about the benefits civilization can provide the Africans. At the inner station he finds that Kurtz is close to death from illness and that although he has acquired a great deal of ivory,

José Gamarra's 1986 oil-on-canvas painting *Five Centuries Later* suggests a pleasant forest in which flora still flourishes, despite the well-paved path that cuts through it, making it hard to decipher whether the disturbances from outside have been beneficial or detrimental. Conrad's somewhat impartial portrayal of imperialism in his classic novella *Heart of Darkness* leaves readers with the same sense of ambiguity.

Kurtz has been raiding the countryside rather than trading. One of the local African tribes follows him and even worships him as a god. A day or so later, they take Kurtz off and head back down river. Kurtz dies along the way, his final words being, "The horror, the horror." Marlow also becomes quite ill and is eventually invalided home. Kurtz had given Marlow some papers before he died; among these are letters from Kurtz's "Intended" (that is, his fiancée). Marlow eventually visits her to return the letters and finds her to be an idealistic person who is unaware of Kurtz's activities in the Congo. Marlow inadvertently lets slip that he heard Kurtz's last words, and when the Intended pushes him to hear what Kurtz said, Marlow tells her that Kurtz whispered her name.

Analysis. *Heart of Darkness* is a somber, brooding, slow-moving tale of discovery: moral discovery, self discovery, and social discovery. Marlow sees rampant amorality and immorality among the Europeans in the African wilderness; he comes to learn that few have the innate strength necessary to maintain moral standards without the external restraints of law and public opinion. Kurtz goes out equipped with the moral ideals of Western civilization, but sometime after arriving in the Congo, his ideals melt away because he is without external restraints and lacks the inner strength to maintain his ideals; in the end he becomes prey to unchecked desire for power, wealth, and control. On a larger scale Marlow discovers that Western civilization, in its various incarnations in the Congo, is either irrelevant or detrimental to the indigenous population. This discovery leads to Marlow's recognizing that Western civilization is not based upon absolute truths but is merely a convenient means for Europeans to organize their social interaction. Nevertheless, in Marlow's lie to Kurtz's Intended, he demonstrates his (also perhaps Conrad's) conflicted views of the role of Western civilization. On the one hand, he comes to accept that it is not based upon absolute truths; on the other hand, he is unwilling to reject it entirely and sees it as a necessary

shelter from the idea of an indifferent universe. Hence, Marlow's lies to the Intended, a pure example of Western civilized ideals, in order not to destroy the world she represents. Ultimately, *Heart of Darkness* requires the reader to question the assumptions of the Western worldview and ask what the purpose of human existence is.

A great deal of debate has arisen regarding whether *Heart of Darkness* supports or rejects European imperialism. Some argue that Conrad's portrayal of the Africans as backward and ignorant amounts to racism and an at least tacit acceptance of the superiority of Western civilization. Others see Conrad's negative portrayal of the Europeans in the Congo as an implicit criticism of imperialist activities. There is solid evidence to support both sides of this issue.

SOURCES FOR FURTHER STUDY

Adams, Richard. *Joseph Conrad: Heart of Darkness*. Penguin Critical Studies. London: Penguin Books, 1991.

Harkness, Bruce, ed. *Conrad's "Heart of Darkness" and the Critics*. San Francisco: Wadsworth, 1960.

Peters, John G. "The Opaque and the Clear: The White Fog Incident in *Heart of Darkness*." *Studies in Short Fiction* 35, no. 4 (fall 1998): 373–386.

LORD JIM

Genre: Novel
Subgenre: Tragic narrative
Published: England, 1900
Time period: 1880s
Setting: Southeast Asia

Themes and Issues. *Lord Jim* considers questions of romantic ideals, notions of honor, the nature of Western civilization, and the nature of one's conception of one's self. Jim gains a view of his abilities from reading romantic fiction, so he sees himself shipwrecked, saving others, and generally being a paragon of heroism. Once he jumps ship, he fails to live up to the ideal expectation he had for himself. He spends the rest of the book trying to prove to himself and others that he is not a coward. The novel considers how human beings develop

The diving figure in *Red Ship,* a 1995 work of oil and acrylic by artist Mary Frank, is reminiscent of Jim's quick departure from those in need in Conrad's 1900 adventure novel, *Lord Jim.* With one swooping jump, Jim's self-esteem plummets and his view of himself is eternally altered.

conceptions of themselves, what makes a hero, and what the cost of heroism is.

The Plot. Charlie Marlow narrates much of the story of Jim, an English officer aboard the *Patna,* a ship carrying Islamic pilgrims to Mecca. One night, the ship hits something and begins to sink. The crew panics and abandons ship, leaving the sleeping passengers. Jim does not take part in the crew's actions, but after the boat has been lowered into the water, he suddenly jumps in. The members of the crew spend several days on the open ocean until a passing ship picks them up. When they arrive ashore, the captain lies about what happened. Unbeknownst to them, the *Patna* did not sink and, though badly damaged, has already been towed ashore. After an official inquiry the crew's

certificates are canceled, and as a result they are barred from further maritime service. Marlow meets Jim during the inquiry and befriends him. Jim is mortified by what he has done and tries to impress upon Marlow that he is not a coward. He later obtains a good position as a water clerk. Sometime afterward one of the crew from the *Patna* shows up, and Jim abruptly leaves his job. This pattern continues: Jim takes a position, something recalls the *Patna* incident, and Jim leaves. Finally, Marlow goes to Stein, a friend and successful trader, about Jim's situation. Stein sends Jim to replace his ineffectual agent Cornelius in Patusan. This opportunity allows Jim to retreat deep into the jungles of an island in the Malaysian archipelago. After arriving, Jim aids Doramin, a local chief, in overthrowing Sherif Ali, another local

SOME INSPIRATIONS BEHIND CONRAD'S WORK

Joseph Conrad was very much influenced by what he read as a youth. In his early years, Victor Hugo, William Shakespeare, Charles Dickens, Miguel de Cervantes Saavedra, James Fenimore Cooper, and Frederick Marryat were among his favorites. In particular, Marryat and Hugo influenced Conrad's fiction. Conrad's lighter sea fiction as well as his Napoleonic fiction ("The Duel," *The Rover,* and *Suspense*) exhibit such influence. Gustave Flaubert and Guy de Maupassant had a more profound influence on Conrad's more serious works.

An even more significant influence on Conrad's works was his personal background. The exile and early death of his parents seem to have soured him on revolutionary politics, and his works exhibit a profound skepticism of such activities. His early orphaning also probably contributed to the dark view that pervades much of his work. Conrad's varied experiences in Russia, Poland, France, England, and the numerous places he visited during his life at sea also greatly influenced his work. Finally, although Conrad is hardly a simple writer of sea fiction, as some have depicted him, his experience on the sea provided the raw material for many of his works and formed much of his thinking about such important themes as solidarity, isolation, and the indifference of nature.

official, who has been oppressing Doramin's people. For quite a while things go well, and Jim becomes Lord Jim, a hero to Doramin's people. Sometime later, however, Gentleman Brown, a fugitive from the law, sails up the river to Patusan and tries to raid Doramin's village. He and his men are repulsed and cornered in a small building. Jim comes to meet him, and Brown convinces Jim to either fight them openly or to let them leave. Doramin thinks that they should simply starve the men out, but Jim convinces him that they should let Brown leave, pledging his own life on the safety of the operation. On their way out, though, Cornelius informs Brown of a small outpost commanded by Doramin's only son. In retribution for his defeat, Brown opens fire on the outpost and kills many men, among them Doramin's son. Jim then goes before Doramin to accept responsibility, and Doramin shoots and kills him.

Analysis. *Lord Jim* is a challenging novel because of Conrad's various changes in time and narrator. The novel investigates how Jim comes to react to the difference between his conception of himself and what he actually is. Jim reads ro-

mantic fiction about heroic rescues at sea and courage in the face of danger and death and sees himself in that light, but reality is contrary to that view. For whatever reason, Jim jumps ship, and because he cannot come to terms with that fact, he spends the rest of his life trying to show he is a hero. Conrad also uses Jim's predicament to subtly criticize Western civilization. Jim's romantic conception of himself is a product of a Western ideal of conduct. By the standards of the romantic literature Jim reads, because he has once failed, he can never be redeemed. He will always be considered a coward. Conrad questions whether the standards are too high or even relevant, whether anyone might not panic, as Jim did, given the right combination of circumstances. Nevertheless, Marlow makes it clear that ideals of conduct, although there may be no absolute truth behind them, are still necessary for a society's adequate functioning. In other words, without the code of conduct, only chaos exists, and so Marlow both accepts and rejects this code.

Marlow is also conflicted in his view of Jim. On the one hand, Jim acts heroically at the end of the novel when he accepts responsibility for his failure, and Marlow seems to admire Jim's action. On the other hand, Jim pays a high price for his courage, a price that perhaps Marlow thinks is too high. In accepting responsibility and death, Jim leaves behind a real relationship, with Jewel, his common-law wife. As Marlow says, "He goes away from a living woman to celebrate his pitiless wedding with a shadowy ideal of conduct." Since in Conrad's world no absolute truths exist, one must wonder whether he approves of such an exchange.

SOURCES FOR FURTHER STUDY

Batchelor, John. *Lord Jim*. London: Unwin Hyman, 1988.

Kuehn, Robert E. *Twentieth-Century Interpretations of "Lord Jim."* Englewood Cliffs, NJ: Prentice-Hall, 1969.

Peters, John G. "Stein's Collection: Order and Chaos in *Lord Jim*." *Conradiana* 28, no. 1 (winter 1996): 48–53.

Tanner, Tony. "Butterflies and Beetles: Conrad's Two Truths" *Chicago Review* 16 (winter-spring 1963): 123–140.

THE SECRET SHARER

Genre: Short story

Subgenre: Initiation tale

Published: England, 1910

Time period: 1880s

Setting: Gulf of Siam

Themes and Issues. "The Secret Sharer" is notable for its investigation of the double, a kind of second self. The new captain learns something of himself as a result of his encounter with his other self, Leggatt. This experience embodies one of the other major issues the story engages: coming to a knowledge of one's self. Conrad presents the captain as unsure of himself in his new position. Untried and untested, the captain wonders whether he is up to the task of commanding a seagoing vessel. The action of the story is meant to answer that question.

The Plot. On the night of his first voyage, a new captain is alone on deck when he notices something at the bottom of the ship's ladder and discovers it is a man. He brings the man aboard unbeknownst to anyone else, and the man, Leggatt, tells the captain that he killed an insubordinate sailor aboard another ship during a storm and that he was arrested for the crime. He escaped and has swum to the captain's ship. The captain shelters Leggatt, who resembles the captain in a variety of ways. After several days the captain offers Leggatt an opportunity to escape, but to do so the captain must steer the ship dangerously close to the island of Koh-Ring. The members of the crew, who have little confidence in their captain, think he has gone mad, but the captain steers them successfully out of danger, using as a marker Leggatt's hat (which fell off when he entered the water).

Thomas Halloran's *Beethoven's Death Mask, Variation #7* mirrors Conrad's themes of duality and self-examination in his 1910 short story, "The Secret Sharer." Conrad often unrelentingly calls on his characters, in this case the captain, to step outside themselves and explore their capabilities objectively, creating the dark possibility and intrigue of discovering something they don't necessarily want to know.

Analysis. Although "The Secret Sharer" lacks the stylistic and narrative complexity of Conrad's earlier works, it is no less intellectually challenging. It is a story that investigates the question of how a man comes to know whether he lives up to the conceptions he has of himself. The new captain is unsure of his abilities, and his crew is also unsure of his abilities. The story demonstrates how the captain comes to grow into his position. In short, it is a story of initiation. As a result of his experience and communion with Leggatt, the new captain discovers that he can make the difficult decisions that one must make to command a vessel, and in fact, by doing so, he becomes the captain of his ship.

The other (though related) major theme in the story has to do with the concept of the double, the idea that there is in each person an opposite side—in many cases, a darker side. Throughout "The Secret Sharer," Conrad reveals similarities between the captain and Leggatt. Leggatt represents the captain's darker self, and the captain learns from his experience with Leggatt and becomes a more fully developed and integrated individual.

Much debate surrounds this story and the captain's decision to harbor Leggatt. Some argue that Conrad sympathizes with the captain's choice in rejecting the unbending rule of law. Others believe that Conrad criticizes the captain's action by emphasizing his disregard for the law and the danger in which he places his own ship. As with so many of the issues Conrad raises in his works, good evidence may be adduced in support of both views.

SOURCES FOR FURTHER STUDY

Harkness, Bruce, ed. *Conrad's "Secret Sharer" and the Critics.* Belmont, CA: Wadsworth, 1962.

Hewitt, Douglas. *Conrad: A Reassessment.* 3rd ed. Totowa, NJ: Rowman and Littlefield, 1975.

Watt, Ian. "'The Secret Sharer': Introduction." In *Essays on Conrad.* Cambridge, UK: Cambridge University Press, 2000, pp. 127–132.

Other Works

NOSTROMO (1904). *Nostromo* is perhaps Conrad's most challenging work; in it he so persistently shifts time that it is nearly impossible to follow the action until one has read more than half of the novel. *Nostromo* was the first of Conrad's political novels and deals with a South American revolution. Costaguana (a mythical South American country) has had relative peace for five years under the liberal dictatorship of Ribiera. A powerful faction led by the Monteros overthrows the government, particularly seeking control of Charles Gould's silver mine in the Sulaco province. During the course of the revolution, however, Sulaco manages to secede.

Nostromo indicts revolution and imperialist capitalism. Conrad shows that the Monteros' goal is wealth and power and that their revolution is no different from the numerous others that have occurred throughout the history of Costaguana. Gould, an Englishman, allows the mine he owns to become all-consuming and to take precedence over his affections for his wife and over the needs of the indigenous people, as the Europeans exploit them in the development of the mine. Besides Gould, the mine destroys Nostromo, head of the dockworkers and a man trusted implicitly for his courage and loyalty to Gould. Nostromo takes a boat carrying a large load of silver out into the gulf during the Monteros' invasion of Sulaco but is nearly swamped by an incoming vessel. He manages to secrete the silver on an island and lets everyone believe that the boat was sunk. His wealth grows slowly, as he takes bar after bar of silver. Later, on one of his trips to the island to retrieve silver, he is mistaken for an intruder and shot to death by his fiancée's father, the lighthouse keeper on the island.

THE SECRET AGENT (1907). *The Secret Agent* is a darkly ironic tale of political espionage and intrigue that recounts an attempted terrorist bomb attack on the Greenwich Observatory in London. Verloc, a secret agent, has grown comfortable while collecting his pay from an unnamed (probably Russian) embassy without having to do much work, but then the new embassy official demands action—specifically, an attempt on the observatory. Verloc botches the attack when his mentally challenged brother-in-law, Stevie, falls while depositing the bomb and blows himself to pieces. Verloc, who has also been serving as a double agent, is eventually discovered by the police, but before the police can arrest him, his wife, Winnie, who has overheard his conversation with the police and learned of her brother's fate, stabs Verloc in the chest with a carving knife and kills him. Winnie later commits suicide.

Verloc is at the center of the anarchist and revolutionary community, and Conrad's attitudes toward anarchism and revolutionary activity are clear in this novel. He presents the anarchists, to a man, as ineffectual and insipid, having no conception of the people for whom they express concern. At the same time the police authorities, with their infighting and intriguing, come off no better. Above all, they cover up Verloc's murder for the sake of saving face, among other things.

Conrad's narrative technique in the novel adds to the political confusion he relates. He moves back and forth in time, and for a good deal of the novel, the reader thinks that Verloc has been blown up rather than Stevie.

UNDER WESTERN EYES (1911). *Under Western Eyes* is the last of Conrad's overtly political novels. Its topic is Russian underground revolutionary activities. Victor Haldin throws a bomb and thereby assassinates a Russian official; he then confesses his act to Razumov, whom he incorrectly believes to be sympathetic to the revolutionary cause. Razumov is afraid of being associated with Haldin, and so he turns him in to the authorities. After Haldin's execution, Razumov becomes a secret agent, largely out of anger for what he sees as a life wrecked by Haldin's visit. Razumov infil-

trates the expatriate Russian revolutionary community in Geneva, Switzerland. During the course of his activities, he falls in love with Haldin's sister, Natalia, and eventually confesses his actions to the revolutionaries. Nikita (who turns out to be a double agent) deafens Razumov in retribution. Unable to hear a street car coming, Razumov is then run over and crippled.

Conrad, who was disdainful of the revolutionaries and their activities in *Nostromo* and *The Secret Agent,* is equally disdainful of those in *Under Western Eyes.* Such actions destroy the lives of innocent bystanders: Razumov, Haldin's mother, and to a certain extent Haldin's sister. Furthermore, the revolutionaries are presented as ineffectual and no better than the regime they seek to overthrow. Nor is Conrad sympathetic to the Russian government, which uses Razumov up and throws him away. Conrad does show sympathy, however, toward displays of compassion and love: Tekla, a somewhat disaffected member of the expatriates, cares for Razumov after his injury, and Razumov decides to give up his scheme of revenge because of his love for Natalia.

THE SHADOW LINE (1917). *The Shadow Line* is often considered Conrad's last great work. It bears some similarity to "The Secret Sharer" in that Conrad based both on his own experience as captain of the *Otago.* A captain takes command of his vessel, and he and the crew set out to sea, but during the voyage they encounter an extended calm period, in which the ship can make no headway toward its destination. To compound matters, the crew becomes quite ill, and the captain discovers that the previous captain removed the ship's store of quinine. The captain's chief mate believes that the ghost of the previous captain has caused the calm. Through the efforts of the members of the crew, despite their illness, the ship eventually makes it out of the calm, and they arrive at their destination.

Like "The Secret Sharer," *The Shadow Line* is a story of initiation, the captain's initiation into manhood and into his profession. The novel is about the intangible line that the initiate must cross before completing the journey and achieving maturity. The young captain is not fully a man nor fully a captain when he assumes command of the ship. During his first voyage he is tested and passes the test as he assumes control of his situation and acts with courage and competence in the face of ongoing bad luck. Conrad suggests that such is the process all individuals must experience as they grow to maturity in any role they fill.

Resources

Cambridge University Press has been publishing a new, critically edited edition of the works of Joseph Conrad. This ongoing project (as of 2003) has enlisted most of the best Conrad scholars in the world. Cambridge is also publishing *The Collected Letters of Joseph Conrad.* Other sources for information of interest on Joseph Conrad include the following:

Joseph Conrad Study Centres. The Polish Social and Cultural Centre in London houses the Joseph Conrad Study Centre, which contains a collection of important Conrad materials. Opole University in Poland has also opened a Joseph Conrad Study Centre, which will be dedicated particularly to Conrad's eastern European experience. The center hopes eventually to establish a Joseph Conrad Museum in Conrad's birthplace.

Joseph Conrad Societies. There are several societies devoted to the study of the works of Joseph Conrad. Each produces a publication. The Joseph Conrad Society of America publishes *Joseph Conrad Today,* a newsletter for the society, and typically sponsors two sessions devoted to Conrad at the annual convention of the Modern Language Association. The Joseph Conrad Society (UK) publishes *The Conradian,* a scholarly journal on Conrad's works that appears twice a year. The Société Conradienne Française publishes *L'epoque conradienne,* an annual journal on Conrad's works. The Polish Conrad Society sponsors an annual, *Con-Texts,* devoted to Conrad studies.

Both the American and British Joseph Conrad Societies sponsor awards supporting the work of emerging scholars. The Joseph Conrad Foundation is another source of material and information on Conrad. Besides the publications of the organizations cited above, the excellent journal *Conradiana* appears three times a year.

Manuscript Collections. Conrad's manuscripts are scattered among a number of libraries. The largest manuscript collections are held at the Beinecke Library at Yale University, the Berg Collection at the New York Public Library, and the Rosenbach Foundation Museum in Philadelphia. Other institutions holding smaller collections of Conrad papers include the Lilly Library at Indiana University, the Harry Ransom Humanities Research Center at the University of Texas at Austin, the Free Library of Philadelphia, the Boston Public Library, the British Library, the Brotherton Collection at Leeds University, the Houghton Library at Harvard University, and the J. Pierpont Morgan Library in New York City.

Web Sites. There is much information about Conrad available to Internet browsers; some is useful, some is not. The Center for Conrad Studies at Kent State University is a good place to start. Simply following the many links from the site will yield hours of erudition and informative pleasure (http://www.library.kent.edu/speccoll/center.html).

JOHN G. PETERS

Tsitsi Dangarembga

BORN: February 14, 1959, Mutoko, Zimbabwe
IDENTIFICATION: Twentieth-century Zimbabwean novelist and film-maker known for her exploration of the struggles of African women against patriarchal values and colonial rule.

SIGNIFICANCE: Tsitsi Dangarembga emerged as a significant writer with the publication of the award-winning novel, *Nervous Conditions,* in 1988. This novel, which concerns a Shona girl whose involvement with her family members is influenced by her education at mission schools, earned Dangarembga critical applause both for her deft creation of engaging characters whose motivations are nuanced and often contradictory and for her ability to expose the complex dynamics, both familial and societal, that systems of colonial domination create. Dangarembga later turned her attention to cinema and, with the release of *Everyone's Child* in 1996, became the first Zimbabwean woman to direct a feature-length film.

The Writer's Life

Childhood. Tsitsi Dangarembga was born on February 14, 1959, in Mutoko, a small town in Zimbabwe, then colonial Rhodesia. From the ages of two to six, she lived in England while her parents attended school there and began her own schooling in the British educational system. As a result, she became fluent in English and lost much of her command of Shona, her native language. Her family returned home when Dangarembga was six. She relearned Shona and was educated first at a missionary school and later at a private American convent school in the city of Mutare, where she prepared for A-level examinations (high-proficiency tests) in mathematics, physics, biology, and chemistry. Dangarembga took up creative writing as a secondary school student, but because of her sheltered upbringing, this very early writing did not reflect the tense political situation developing in Rhodesia at the time.

The Fledgling Writer. In 1977 Dangarembga traveled to Cambridge, England, to study medicine. She had a difficult time being so far from her home in Africa and was shocked by what seemed to her the ethnocentrism of English society. She returned to Zimbabwe in 1980 just before independence. While in England she produced a collection of unpublished poetry, and her intention upon her return home was to work in the literary and dramatic arts. She took a position as a copywriter in an advertising agency in Harare to support herself and began to work on her own writing in earnest. After leaving the agency two years later, she compiled a portfolio of three plays: *Baines Avenue Way, Out of Exile,* and *Tobias Makombe.* All of

This photograph, which captures members of the Shona group posing for the camera on Mount Darwin, in northeastern Zimbabwe, epitomizes the culture and rural existence into which Dangarembga was born in 1959.

this material was sent to a publishing house in Harare, but it was returned to her a year later.

At the age of 22, Dangarembga enrolled in the bachelor's degree program in psychology at the University of Zimbabwe. Here she contributed to the student magazine *Focus* and coauthored a drama. She also became a member of the newly revived drama group Zambuko. Finding few plays with suitable roles for African women, Dangarembga wrote several dramas (including *She No Longer Weeps, The Lost of the Soil,* and *The Third One*), two of which were put into production by the club. These productions were received with great enthusiasm, for the audiences enjoyed the novelty of seeing identifiable characters speaking a language they could understand. The success of these productions encouraged Dangarembga to compile another portfolio of plays and submit it to local publishers. Again, she received no positive response.

Nevertheless, Dangarembga continued to write. In 1985, when she was 25 years old, her short story "The Letter" was published in Sweden, and she finished work on her first novel, *Nervous Conditions.* She submitted the novel to her Zimbabwean publishing contacts, but after many months the manuscript was returned. As a result, Dangarembga was convinced she could not write and became ill. Finally, she submitted the manuscript to the Women's Press in London. The waiting period that followed was extremely difficult for her, even though she had the support of other Zimbabwean writers, including Stephen Chifunyise, a playwright and the head of the university's drama department, and the novelists Wilson Katiyo, Chenjerai Hove, and Shimmer Chinodya.

Recognition at Last. Dangarembga then pursued postgraduate studies and began teach-

These female students working in a laboratory at the University of Zimbabwe in the latter half of the twentieth century exemplify Dangarembga's early pursuits in science and depict a world Dangarembga ultimately left behind when she made the initially shaky decision to pursue a writing career.

ing psychology at the university. In 1987 her play *She No Longer Weeps* was published by the College Press of Zimbabwe, and finally *Nervous Conditions,* published by the Women's Press, appeared in 1988, almost four years after its completion. It was later published by the Seattle-based Seal Press. *Nervous Conditions* was the first novel to be written by a black Zimbabwean woman, and in 1989 it won Dangarembga the African section of the Commonwealth Writers Prize. This award was preceded by the second-place prize she received in a short story competition in Sweden.

Film Directing. After the release and astonishing success of *Nervous Conditions,* Dangarembga intended to continue writing novels, perhaps even a sequel to the first novel. However, the difficulties of publishing as a woman writer in Africa caused her to turn her talents toward filmmaking instead. In 1989 she decided to go to Berlin to study film direction at the Deutsche Film- und Fernseh-Akademie. While in school she made many films, including a documentary for German television. This extended stay in Germany did not distance Dangarembga from her homeland; she maintained a strong sense of African identity, as was demonstrated in 1996, when she was commissioned by Media for Development Trust (MFD) to be part of a writing team chosen to adapt a short story by Shimmer Chinodya for the screen and, more important, to direct the full-length film. The resulting production, entitled *Everyone's Child,* which depicts four siblings in Zimbabwe who have lost their parents to AIDS, has been shown worldwide at various film festivals. Dangarembga was the first black Zimbabwean woman to direct a feature film.

HIGHLIGHTS IN DANGAREMBGA'S LIFE

1959	Tsitsi Dangarembga is born in Mutoko, Rhodesia.
1961	Lives in England and begins her schooling in the British educational system.
1965	Returns to Rhodesia with her family and completes primary and secondary education in Mutare.
1977	Travels to Cambridge, England, to study medicine.
1980	Returns to Rhodesia shortly before the country's independence.
1981	Enrolls in bachelor's degree program in psychology at the University of Zimbabwe; writes several dramas.
1985	Finishes *Nervous Conditions* and submits it to various publishers.
1987	*She No Longer Weeps* is published.
1988	*Nervous Conditions* is published.
1989	Dangarembga wins the African section of the Commonwealth Writers Prize.
1989	Moves to Berlin to study film directing.
1996	Directs the film *Everyone's Child,* written by Shimmer Chinodya.

NERVOUS CONDITIONS

BY TSITSI DANGAREMBGA
INCLUDES AN INTERVIEW WITH THE AUTHOR

"That rare novel whose characters are unforgettable. It is an expression of liberation not to be missed."—Alice Walker

Issues in Dangarembga's Fiction. While Dangarembga has worked in film and drama, her novel, *Nervous Conditions,* has gained her the most critical attention. The most conspicuous qualities of this work are its complex characters and its sophisticated understanding of the interrelationships between colonialism and patriarchy. In this exploration of colonial Rhodesia, white characters are almost nonexistent; rather, Dangarembga considers the effects of institutions created by the colonial government by examining the dynamics within the African community itself.

People in Dangarembga's Fiction. Dangarembga depicts very realistic and multifaceted characters with psychological dimensions that they themselves are not aware of. This complexity is seen in the character of Babamukuru, the patriarch of the novel and the headmaster of a mission school, who represents the forces of colonialism while also embracing his traditional role as the eldest male of an extended Shona family. Similarly, Ma´Shingayi, the mother of the novel's protagonist, proclaims that a woman must carry the burdens of her gender with strength. At the same time, she seethes over the laziness of the men and gives her daughter permission to raise her own school fees so as to continue her educa-

tion. The most obvious example of contradiction is Nyasha, the protagonist's cousin, who is a self-proclaimed hybrid thanks to her early years in England and her adolescence in Rhodesia. The protagonist, Tambu, must also contend with the conflicting values that emerge in her own person when she leaves the village to be educated by missioners, supposedly in an effort to save her family from the rural poverty that has entrapped them.

The many components that come together to form an image in Wadsworth Jarrell's 1971 acrylic-on-canvas painting *Revolutionary* reflect the need for change, demonstrated by Dangarembga's innovative character Nyasha and the rich, complex, and diverse facets of all of Dangarembga's characters in her novel, *Nervous Conditions,* the first novel to be written by a black Zimbabwean woman—Dangarembga's own revolutionary feat.

Gender Discrimination. The theme of gender discrimination is pervasive throughout Dangarembga's work. The women of *Nervous Conditions* are restricted in the education they can receive, the ways they can spend their money, and the manner in which they can express themselves without being thought immoral. This bias affects all the women, regardless of educational status or class affiliation, but the bonding the women experience as fellow victims of male dominance ultimately assists them in coping with the roles they are expected to play. *Nervous Conditions* features two pairings of female characters who support and encourage one another—most obviously, Tambu and Nyasha but also Tambu's mother and her sister, Lucia. Some hope also exists in the fact that many of the women commit small acts of disobedience or rebellion by the novel's close and thereby achieve some measure of personal liberation.

BIBLIOGRAPHY

Bardolph, Jacqueline. "'The Tears of Childhood' of Tsitsi Dangarembga." *Commonwealth Essays and Studies* 13, no. 1 (1990): 91–100.

Bravman, Bill, and Mary Montgomery. "Tsitsi Dangarembga's *Nervous Conditions*." In *African Novels in the Classroom,* edited by Margaret Hay. Boulder: Lynne Rienner, 2000, pp. 97–106.

George, Rosemary Marangoly, and Helen Scott. "An Interview with Tsitsi Dangarembga." *Novel* (spring 1993): 309–319.

McWilliams, Sally. "Tsitsi Dangarembga's *Nervous Conditions:* At the Crossroads of Feminism and Post-colonialism." *World Literature Written in English* 31, no. 1 (1991): 103–112.

Schatteman, Renée. "Fanon and Beyond: The 'Nervous Condition' of the Colonized Woman." *Beyond Survival: African Literature and the Search for New Life,* edited by Kofi Anyidolio. Trenton, NJ: Africa World Press, 1999, pp. 207–216.

Thomas, Sue. "Killing the Hysteric in the Colonized's House: Tsitsi Dangarembga's *Nervous Conditions.*" *The Journal of Commonwealth Literature* 27, no. 1 (1992): 26–36.

Uwakweh, Pauline A. "Debunking Patriarchy: The Liberational Quality of Voicing in Tsitsi Dangarembga's *Nervous Conditions.*" *Research in African Literatures* 26, no. 1 (summer 1995): 75–84.

Veit-Wild, Flora. "Interview with Dangarembga: Women Write about Things That Move Them." *Matatu: Zeitschrift für afrikanische Kultur und Gesellschaft* 3, no. 6 (1989): 101–108.

Wilkinson, Jane. "Interview with Dangarembga." In *Talking with African Writers.* London: Heinemann, 1990, pp. 188–198.

Untitled Suit, Whitfield Lovell's 1992 work of oil and charcoal on paper, embodies the desire of the female characters in Dangarembga's *Nervous Conditions,* her 1988 award-winning work of fiction, to emerge from a male-dominated world. Gender discrimination is a prominent theme in Dangarembga's work in general, but it is particularly so in *Nervous Conditions.*

Reader's Guide to Major Works

NERVOUS CONDITIONS

Genre: Novel
Subgenre: Feminist bildungsroman
Published: Seattle, 1988
Time period: 1960s and 1970s
Setting: Umtali, Rhodesia

Themes and Issues. *Nervous Conditions* addresses the effects of Western education in Africa, the restrictions upon women's freedoms under a patriarchal social structure, and the interconnections between racial and gender discrimination. Most apparent is the theme of gender bias. Tambu resents that "the needs and sensibilities of the women in my family were not considered a priority, or even legitimate." Dangarembga's critique of colonialism is also pervasive, though the novel contains only one reference to the political situation with the mention of the 1965 Unilateral Declaration of Independence, when white Rhodesians broke from the British to avoid a majority-rule government. This action provoked the 14-year liberation struggle that serves as the novel's unacknowledged backdrop.

The Plot. The novel opens with Tambu declaring, "I was not sorry when my brother died." This brother, Nhamo, died while attending the mission school run by Babamukuru. Nhamo's family had hoped his education would allay their poverty. Tambu resented the opportunities given Nhamo because of his gender and feels vindicated when, after his death, she is sent to the mission.

Overwhelmed by the mission's luxury, Tambu wonders how she will fit in, but she is greeted warmly by her cousin Nyasha. Tambu is grateful for her uncle's hospitality and obeys his demand to study diligently. She proves to be very successful and reads a lot of fiction, mostly by British writers. By contrast, Nyasha

The limpness of the woman in Jacob Lawrence's 1985 painting *Dreams No. 2* (Smithsonian American Art Museum, Washington, D.C.) suggests the comatose-like state of Tambu in Dangarembga's highly acclaimed 1988 novel, *Nervous Conditions,* as she undergoes an out-of-body experience, from which she emerges with an unveiled strength to refuse to stand on ceremony at her parents' arranged wedding and the determination to oppose her influential uncle.

prefers "real" topics, such as apartheid and the Unilateral Declaration of Independence. Tambu tries to avoid the anglicized and disrespectful Nyasha but grows to love her despite their differences. One night a physical fight ensues between Babamukuru and Nyasha after he accuses her of being a whore. Instead of taking sides, Tambu abstains, hiding behind the role of a "grateful, poor female relative."

When visiting the village, Tambu realizes that the homestead is filthy and there are many problems in her family. Lucia, Tambu's aunt, has become pregnant by a married cousin of Tambu's father. Babamukuru believes this family trouble is occurring because Tambu's parents were never properly married, and he plans to give them a church wedding. Tambu fears that her parents will be reduced to comic figures, and on the morning of the ceremony, she cannot get out of bed. She has an out-of-body experience as Babamukuru yells at her but voices her refusal once she slips back into her body.

Later Tambu accepts an offer to attend a convent school run by European nuns; Nyasha worries her cousin will become too assimilated, and her mother becomes ill at the news. Before leaving, Tambu dines at the mission and watches as Babamukuru forces his daughter to eat. Nyasha complies and then goes to the bathroom and vomits.

Tambu throws herself into life at the convent. When Nyasha writes that she misses Tambu badly, Tambu resolves to write back but finds no time. During term break, Tambu discovers that Nyasha appears skeletal from her nightly vomiting. Soon after, Nyasha has a nervous breakdown; she shreds her history book and blames the colonialists for taking the African people away from themselves. The family takes her to a white psychiatrist, who says that Africans cannot suffer from anorexia nervosa. Another psychiatrist agrees to put her into a clinic to get rest.

Tambu's mother proclaims the problem with Nyasha is her "Englishness." Tambu wonders if she too is being altered by her education. She returns to the convent but no longer sees it as a "sunrise" on her horizon. Something in her mind begins to assert itself and to question things. This reflective process eventually enables her to tell the story of the four women she loves—Nyasha, Maiguru, Lucia, and her mother.

Analysis. The title and epigraph of Dangarembga's novel are taken from the introduction to *The Wretched of the Earth* by Frantz Fanon

SOME INSPIRATIONS BEHIND DANGAREMBGA'S WORK

Dangarembga speaks of the therapeutic quality of storytelling, suggesting that her impulse to write came out of personal pain. She began to record her feelings during secondary school, a time when she experienced isolation. Later she turned to poetry in reaction to the loneliness and homesickness she felt at Cambridge when studying medicine. By the time she decided to return to Zimbabwe, she knew she wanted to give up her scientific leanings and do creative work instead. Her involvement with theater at the University of Zimbabwe prompted her to further her interest in playwriting, and this experience eventually led to her work with the novel form. Dangarembga claims that the greatest literary influences on her writing were African American women writers (such as Toni Morrison, Alice Walker, and Maya Angelou), who taught her something about herself and her context, and African writers (such as Chinua Achebe and Ngũgĩ wa Thiong'o), who pointed her in the direction of literature from her own continent.

FICTION	DRAMA	FILM
1988 Nervous Conditions	1987 She No Longer Weeps	1996 Everyone's Child

(1925–1961), the French psychiatrist and theorist of revolution. *Nervous Conditions* echoes Fanon's belief that the illogic of racial supremacy plays upon the nerves of a colonized people. There is evidence of disturbed nerves in all the characters. Tambu experiences deep psychological crisis. She has clearly been influenced by Western education—she reads British writers, worships the well-educated Babamukuru, and as a result feels disdain for village life—but she also has been influenced by Nyasha to defend her racial identity. The coexistence of eager imitation and angry defense results in a dangerous internal division, as is seen when she must separate her mind from her body to refuse Babamukuru's demand that she attend the wedding.

However, the conclusion promises that, despite her mission education, Tambu will survive with her African identity intact. She has been through a long, painful process of expansion, moving from her early adoration of Babamukuru to the protest of her parents' marriage and finally to the understanding that enables her to pen the story of her family.

SOURCES FOR FURTHER STUDY

Fanon, Frantz. *Black Skin White Masks*. London: Grove, 1967.
—-. *The Wretched of the Earth*. New York: Grove, 1963.

Other Works

EVERYONE'S CHILD (1996). This film, funded by Zimbabwe's Media for Development Trust (MFD), a production company that focuses on urgent social issues, was directed by Dangarembga. She also assisted in writing the screen adaptation, which is based on a short story written by Simmer Chinodya, author of *Harvest of Thorns*. The film presents four siblings who lose their parents to AIDS and are consequently neglected by everyone in their village. Even their uncle and guardian violates his customary responsibilities by selling their farming equipment and offering them no assistance. In desperation the oldest brother travels to Harare to find a job and send money home, but he ends up joining a gang of homeless boys and getting arrested instead. Left alone with the two youngsters in her care, the oldest sister is forced to accept the self-serving generosity of a lecherous shopkeeper. The other villagers ostracize her for being a prostitute until the night when the girl is forced to accompany the shopkeeper to a nightclub and the youngest child dies in a

Under the direction of Dangarembga, the 1996 film *Everyone's Child* addresses the struggles of a small, time-honored community to keep up with a constantly transforming African society. The child actors reveal the destitution of the orphaned and diseased children, who are at the mercy of their uncle and their neighbors. With the release of *Everyone's Child*, Dangarembga became the first Zimbabwean woman to direct a feature-length film.

house fire. The uncle and the villagers feel shame over their neglect, and they help the remaining children rebuild their lives.

Everyone's Child reminds viewers of the traditional practice of caring for orphans in a community, a practice forgotten in recent years with the shocking rise in the number of orphans. By illustrating the wider societal content of the disease, the film also demonstrates that women and children are the ones most affected when a community experiences a large-scale crisis such as AIDS.

Resources

A documentary entitled *Frantz Fanon: Black Skin White Masks* provides a thorough explanation of the anticolonial theories of Frantz Fanon and is available for rental or purchase from California Newsreel (www.newsreel.org). Fanon's theories consider the psychological impact of racism on both the colonizer and the colonized and therefore provide important insights into the human dynamics that Dangarembga explores in *Nervous Conditions*. Dangarembga's film, *Everyone's Child,* is also available through California Newsreel.

In addition, there are a number of Internet sites that provide biographical, contextual, and critical material on Dangarembga's work.

African Authors. This site, based at Central Oregon Community College, contains background information about a wide array of African writers, as well as many useful links (www.cocc.edu/cagatucci/classes/hum211/dangarembga.htm).

Postcolonial and Postimperial Literature. This Singapore-based site has one of the most comprehensive sets of links to articles and information on Dangarembga to be found on the Web (www.scholars.nus.edu.sg/landow/post/zimbabwe/td/dangarembgaov.html).

Postcolonial Studies. This Emory University site includes a brief biography and links to other postcolonial writers (www.emory.edu/ENGLISH/Bahri/Dangar.html).

Tsitsi Dangarembga. This excellent site is the work of the African literature department at the University of Western Australia (www.arts.uwa.edu.au/AFLIT/DangarembgaEN.html).

RENÉE T. SCHATTEMAN

Anita Desai

BORN: June 24, 1937, Mussoorie, India

IDENTIFICATION: Twentieth-century Indian novelist best known for her psychological novels about lonely and unhappy people, one of which has been made into a film and another into a miniseries for television.

SIGNIFICANCE: Anita Desai is one of the best-known and finest Indian novelists writing in English. Though most of her books explore what she sees as the oppression of women within marriage and family and their struggle for identity and independence, her larger focus is on the isolation experienced by those who live outside the mainstream of society. Her supreme mastery lies in her ability to convey the atmosphere that surrounds the characters and reflects their state of mind. Three of Desai's novels, *Clear Light of Day* (1980), *In Custody* (1984), and *Fasting, Feasting* (1999), were nominated for the Booker Prize, the most prestigious British literary award.

The Writer's Life

Anita Mazumdar Desai was born in a hill station in the state of Uttar Pradesh in northern India. Her father, D. N. Mazumdar, a Bengali businessman, met her mother, Toni Nime, a German, when he was a student in Germany. After getting married, they went to India in the late 1920s. The fact that her mother was European had a major impact on Desai's fiction. Her mother's perceptions about Indian culture enabled Desai to look at India both as an outsider and as an Indian.

Childhood. Desai, by and large, is a person who guards her privacy, and what is known about her life derives from her interviews. Desai grew up in Delhi, in a house, garden, and neighborhood similar to the one she describes in her novel *Clear Light of Day,* which, she says, is the most autobiographical of all her novels. She also grew up speaking three languages, German, Hindi, and English. Her parents spoke German at home, so it was the first language she learned. She spoke Hindi to friends

Normally private, Desai was thrice thrust into the spotlight when she was nominated for the Booker Prize, the most esteemed British literary award. She received the first nomination for *Clear Light of Day,* which was published in 1980, the same year this photograph was taken.

and neighbors and learned English at school. Since she did most of her reading in English, it was the language she was most fluent in, and thus, writing in it came naturally to Desai.

The Future Writer. Desai grew up in a middle-class home, a house that was full of books, along with two older sisters and a brother. One sister became a civil servant and the other a pediatrician. All the siblings were avid readers; they were always going to the library and the bookshop. After Desai was taught how to read and write at school, she decided that she wanted to be a writer and started writing at the age of seven. At the age of nine, after having her first story published in an American children's magazine, she was labeled the writer of the family and has been a writer ever since.

After graduating from Queen Mary's Higher Secondary School in 1954, Desai attended Miranda House, an elite college of Delhi University, where she obtained a bachelor of

FILMS BASED ON DESAI'S STORIES

1992 *The Village by the Sea* (BBC miniseries)

1993 *In Custody*

The late eighties marked a dramatic shift in Desai's life. She left India in 1986 to become a visiting fellow at Girton College, part of Cambridge University in England. The following year she embarked on her teaching career in the United States.

HIGHLIGHTS IN DESAI'S LIFE

1937   Anita Mazumdar is born on June 24 in Mussoorie, India.

1957   Graduates from Miranda House, Delhi University; publishes first short story.

1957–1958 Works at Max Mueller Bhavan, a German-language cultural center, in Calcutta.

1958   Marries Ashvin Desai.

1958–1962 Lives in Calcutta.

1963   Publishes first novel, *Cry, the Peacock.*

1965   Makes first trip to England.

1977   Publishes *Fire on the Mountain,* which receives the Indian National Academy of Letters (the Sahitya Akademi) Award and the British Royal Society of Literature's Winifred Holtby Memorial Prize.

1980   Publishes *Clear Light of Day,* which is nominated for the Booker Prize.

1982   Publishes *The Village by the Sea,* which receives the Guardian Award for children's fiction.

1984   Publishes *In Custody;* nominated for the Booker Prize.

1986–1987 Is visiting Fellow at Girton College, Cambridge University; writes *Baumgartner's Bombay;* these years mark the beginning of Desai's move away from India.

1987   Desai moves to America.

1990   Is awarded the title Padma Shri (highest civilian honor) by the government of India.

1999   Publishes *Fasting, Feasting,* which is nominated for the Booker Prize.

BOOKER PRIZE FINALIST

ANITA DESAI

FASTING FEASTING

a novel by the author of BAUMGARTNER'S BOMBAY

"Desai is more than smart; she's an undeniable genius."
— WASHINGTON POST BOOK WORLD

"Poignant, penetrating . . . a splendid novel."
— WALL STREET JOURNAL

arts degree in English literature in 1957. She also published her first short story the same year.

Marriage and Domestic Life.
After college Desai worked for a year at the Max Mueller Bhavan, a German-language institute and cultural center in Calcutta, before getting married on December 13, 1958, to Ashvin Desai, a business executive. It would be nearly 30 years before Desai would take a job again, as a professor of creative writing at Smith College. Desai had two sons, Rahul and Arjun, and two daughters, Tani and Kiran, by the time she was 34. Writing and taking care of a family posed no problem for her. She stayed at home and learned to write around her children's schedules. She had a desk in her bedroom to which she would go immediately when the children were in school or at play. (Her youngest child, her daughter Kiran, published her own first novel, *Hullabaloo in the Guava Orchard,* in 1998 to rave reviews.)

The Fledgling Writer.
Desai wrote her first novel in 1960 but was not able to publish it till three years later because Indian publishers were unwilling to take on an unknown writer. Desai was published in India only after her first two novels, *Cry, the Peacock* (1963) and *Voices in the City* (1965), were published in England.

Writing Successes.
The book that made Desai world-famous and won her critical acclaim was her sixth novel, *Clear Light of Day.* The Booker Prize nomination it received brought it to the attention of the literary world. Desai followed *Clear Light of Day* with other writing successes. In 1982 Desai's novel for children, *The Village by the Sea,* received the Guardian Award for children's fiction and was adapted in 1992 as a six-part miniseries by the British Broadcasting Corporation (BBC). *In Custody* was Desai's second novel to be nominated for the Booker Prize and was made into a film, for which Desai helped write the screenplay. For her next novel, *Baumgartner's Bombay* (1988), Desai received the Hadassah Award.

Moving to America.
In 1986 Desai left India to take up the position of a visiting fellow at Girton College, Cambridge University, where she wrote *Baumgartner's Bombay.* This period marked the beginning of her move away from India. She taught at Smith College in 1987 and 1988 and at Mount Holyoke College from 1988 to 1993. In 1993 she accepted a position teaching creative writing at the Massachusetts Institute of Technology. Desai subsequently wrote two novels, *Journey to Ithaca* (1995) and *Fasting, Feasting* (1999), the second of which won Desai her third Booker nomination, and a book of short stories, *Diamond Dust: Stories* (2000).

Desai's teaching position at the Massachusetts Institute of Technology, which she accepted in 1993, was the first professional appointment by the university in fiction writing in twenty years. In a colloquium entitled "How Do Artists Tell Their Stories?" at MIT in 2001, Desai compared her life in India, which involved years of reflection and contemplation, with her role as teacher, which she said makes her "more analytical."

The Writer's Work

Anita Desai has written long and short fiction, for both adults and children, and nonfiction. She is, however, known primarily for her long fiction about the inner lives of middle-class women and men. The most remarkable quality about her writing is her precise description of the landscape and her sympathy for the misfits of society.

Issues in Desai's Fiction. A sense of pessimism pervades all of Desai's novels because they deal with the loneliness of existence and with the ways in which individuals are trapped within society. Most of Desai's early novels, *Cry, the Peacock, Voices in the City, Where Shall We Go This Summer?* (1975), *Fire on the Mountain* (1977), and *Clear Light of Day,* and her most recent one, *Fasting, Feasting,* focus on women who are confined by traditional roles that are prescribed by their culture. Although Desai shifted her focus from female to male characters in *In Custody* and *Baumgartner's Bombay,* she does not portray the men as stronger individuals in comparison with women; her men, too, are vulnerable people, overwhelmed with a sense of helplessness and hopelessness.

Descriptive Imagery. A major element of Desai's fiction is her use of descriptive words to convey the atmosphere that reflects the minds and motivations of individuals. For example, in *Clear Light of Day,* the dry, hot Indian climate, con-

veyed through the imagery of the scorching sun and the dust storms, reflects the anger and bitterness inside Bim. In *Cry, the Peacock* the monsoon thunderstorms reflect the inner emotions of Maya when she unleashes the "storms" raging within her.

Desai, seen here in 1991, likened writing to "the activity of a fisherwoman sending line down to the depths. The writer must believe that in that lake there is a fish. Ripples can be seen. Even the cruising fin is there for all to see. But what sets the writer apart is belief in the body of a fish living just below the surface. Writing is a way to explore what lies below."

People in Desai's Fiction. Desai's strongest fictional characters are the defeated and unsuccessful people of this world: those who are unable to confront the world, like Hugo Baumgartner in *Baumgartner's Bombay*; who are unable to take on life's challenges, like Uma in *Fasting, Feasting*; who are gullible, like Deven in *In Custody*; and who seek to isolate themselves, like Nanda Kaul in *Fire on the Mountain*.

BIBLIOGRAPHY

Afzal-Khan, Fawzia. *Cultural Imperialism and the Indo-English Novel: Genre and Ideology in the Novels of R. K. Narayan, Anita Desai, Kamala Markandaya and Salman Rushdie*. University Park: Pennsylvania State University, 1993.

Budholia, O. P. *Anita Desai: Vision and Technique in Her Novels*. Delhi: B. R. Publishers, 2001.

Chatterjee, Chandra. *Surviving Colonialism: A Study of R. K. Narayan, Anita Desai, V. S. Naipaul*. Antwerp: Universiteit Antwerpen, 2000.

Griffiths, Sian, ed. *Beyond the Glass Ceiling: Forty Women Whose Ideas Shape the Modern World*. Manchester, UK: Manchester University Press, 1996.

Jain, Jasbir. *Stairs to the Attic: The Novels of Anita Desai*. Jaipur, India: Printwell, 1987. 2nd ed., 1999.

Jussawalla, Feroza, and Reed Way Dasenbrock, eds. *Interviews with Writers of the Post-Colonial World*. Jackson: University Press of Mississippi, 1992.

Mukherjee, Meenakshi. *The Twice-Born Fiction*. New Delhi: Arnold-Heinemann, 1972.

Parker, Michael, and Roger Starkey, eds. *Postcolonial Literatures: Achebe, Ngugi, Desai, Walcott*. New York: St. Martin's Press, 1995.

SOME INSPIRATIONS BEHIND DESAI'S WORK

The greatest influence on Desai has been her mother, from whom Desai learned to look at India with the eyes of an outsider and who has played a major role in shaping Desai's critical perceptions about Indian culture. Also from her mother, Desai heard stories about Germany, nursery rhymes and fairytales, a part of her heritage that Desai drew from for the first time in her novel *Baumgartner's Bombay*.

Desai acknowledges the influences on her work of Virginia Woolf, D. H. Lawrence, Albert Camus, Anton Chekhov, and Henry James. One can also find echoes of E. M. Forster's *A Passage to India* (1924) in the cave scene in *Baumgartner's Bombay*.

Another major influence on Desai has been her friend and mentor, the novelist and screenwriter Ruth Prawer Jhabvala, who, like Desai's mother, was a German immigrant married to an Indian. Jhabvala's influence is clearly visible in Desai's novel *A Journey to Ithaca*, which delves into the lives of Europeans looking to India for spiritual enlightenment.

Writer Ruth Prawer Jhabvala (left), Desai's great friend and mentor, arrives at a memorabilia auction to benefit the Film Foundation in New York with director James Ivory and producer Ismail Merchant on July 27, 1999.

CLEAR LIGHT OF DAY

Genre: Novel
Subgenre: Psychological-realist fiction
Published: London, 1980
Time period: 1940s–1970s
Setting: Old Delhi

Themes and Issues. *Clear Light of Day* focuses on the roles of wives, mothers, sisters, daughters, and widows within families. Central to the story is the importance of the family and of maintaining family relationships. The novel also explores the role of memory in keeping old wounds alive. The clearing up of misunderstandings between family members by the reevaluation of those memories, the novel shows, can help bring about reconciliation.

The Plot. Tara is home in India, on vacation from Washington, D.C., visiting her sister, Bim, in Delhi after three years. Bim, who is independent and unmarried, is a professor of history at a Delhi college. She takes care of the family business and of her autistic brother, Baba. An older brother, Raja, married Benazir, their wealthy neighbor's daughter, and moved away. Tara married Bakul, whose job in the foreign service keeps her away. The four siblings grew up in a family with absent parents who preferred playing bridge at their club. When Raja and Tara leave home, Bim feels abandoned by both.

Bim's bitterness toward Raja, her older brother, stems from the fact that, after marrying Benazir, the daughter of their wealthy neighbor, Hyder Ali, Raja writes a letter to Bim as the new landlord. Bim has continued to live in the house that her family rented from Hyder Ali. However, upon Hyder Ali's death, the ownership of his house passes to his only daughter. Given the fact that in Indian culture the older brother, next to the father, plays the role of a protector, Raja's letter angers Bim and adds to her resentment for being abandoned by Raja. Tara helps in the reconciliation of her brother and sister after she clears up childhood misunderstandings between herself and Bim.

Analysis. *Clear Light of Day* is a critique of the treatment of wives and widows in a patriarchal culture, with the submissive wife, Tara, and the widowed, selfless Aunt Mira as emblematic figures. The novel is also critical of the selfless role that a sister is expected to play in such a culture. Bim, the heroine, rejects marriage for independence. Nevertheless, she plays the culturally acceptable role of the sister who stays on in the family home, looks after her sick brother, and takes care of the family business.

Victoria Skinner's untitled work encapsulates the two separate worlds of Bim, the protagonist in Desai's *Clear Light of Day.* On one hand, Bim is like a prisoner held captive in her suffocating role as dutiful sister, caretaker of the home, and head of the family business. On the other hand, she is the only one who can find comfort in choosing independence for herself. In *Clear Light of Day,* Desai explores the injustice of India's patriarchal culture and the importance of familial love and loyalty.

Like Bim, her neighbors, the Misra sisters, work hard running a nursery school at home during the day and giving music and dance lessons in the evenings to look after their two lazy brothers. The novel also shows how parental neglect and a lack of love draw children to others for attention and warmth. Tara, for example, spends her time with the Misra family, and Raja seeks the company of the Hyder family. The novel thus emphasizes the importance of love in maintaining family relationships.

SOURCES FOR FURTHER STUDY

Bande, Usha. *The Novels of Anita Desai: A Study in Character and Conflict.* New Delhi: Prestige Books, 1988.

Bliss, Corinne Demas. "Against the Current: A Conversation with Anita Desai." *Massachusetts Review* 29, no. 3 (fall 1988): 521–537.

BAUMGARTNER'S BOMBAY

Genre: Novel
Subgenre: Psychological-realist fiction
Published : New York, 1988
Time period: 1930s–1980s
Setting: Bombay, Calcutta, and New Delhi, India

Themes and Issues. Desai had always wanted to find a way to draw on her German heritage, her German childhood, and her knowledge of the German language. *Baumgartner's Bombay*, considered her masterpiece by some critics, allows Desai to use the German strand of her life. In the story of Hugo Baumgartner's 50 years in India, Desai also explores the theme of the outsider, someone outside the mainstream of society, whose suffering Desai sees as part of the human condition.

The Plot. The plot of *Baumgartner's Bombay* is a simple one: Hugo Baumgartner, a German Jew, arrives in India before World War II to escape the Nazis. Even though he becomes a citizen of India, he is always perceived as a foreigner. Baumgartner befriends Kurt, a young, sick man, a German tourist in India. Kurt, a drug addict, kills Hugo Baumgartner for the silver cups that Hugo had won at horse races.

Analysis. Desai's primary purpose in creating the character of Hugo Baumgartner was to draw on the German part of her background, especially her mother's memories of prewar Germany, from which stem the scenes from Hugo's childhood with his mother. Desai wanted to bring to life the bedtime stories her mother told of her childhood in Berlin. Desai's other purpose in this novel is to convey the predicament of an immigrant who is not accepted. She examines India through Hugo, who never feels at ease in that country and who is baffled by the culture, the food, the people, and the climate. As a human being, Hugo is painted as a pitiful character with no control over his life. The rejection of his identity everywhere he

---

NOVELS

1963 Cry, the Peacock
1965 Voices in the City
1971 Bye-Bye, Blackbird
1975 Where Shall We Go This Summer?
1977 Fire on the Mountain
1980 Clear Light of Day
1984 In Custody
1988 Baumgartner's Bombay
1995 Journey to Ithaca
1999 Fasting, Feasting

FICTION FOR CHILDREN

1974 The Peacock Garden
1976 Cat on a Houseboat
1982 The Village by the Sea

SHORT FICTION COLLECTIONS

1978 Games at Twilight and Other Stories
2000 Diamond Dust: Stories

ESSAYS

1984 "The Indian Writer's Problems"
1989 "Indian Fiction Today"
1991 "India: The Seed of Destruction"
1994 "Re-reading Tagore"
1995 "Bellow, the Rain King"
1995 "Publishers, Agents, and Agendas"
1996 "A Coat of Many Colors"

goes makes Baumgartner a lost man, without enthusiasm or desire for attachment.

SOURCES FOR FURTHER STUDY

Bliss, Corinne Demas. "Against the Current: A Conversation with Anita Desai." *Massachusetts Review* 29, no. 3 (fall 1988): 521–537.

Libert, Florence. "An Interview with Anita Desai, 1 August 1989. Cambridge. England." *World Literature Written in English* 30, no. 1 (1990): 47–55.

Newman, Judie. "History and Letters: Anita Desai's Baumgartner's Bombay." *World Literature Written in English* 30, no. 1 (1990): 37–46.

Other Works

FIRE ON THE MOUNTAIN (1977). *Fire on the Mountain* weaves together the lives of three female characters. The protagonist, Nanda Kaul, is living in self-imposed isolation in Carignano, a house on a quiet hillside in Kasauli, a Himalayan hill station. Her solitude is disturbed when Raka, her nine-year-old great-granddaughter, is sent to spend a summer with her. Her privacy is further invaded when Ila Das, Nanda Kaul's old college friend, comes to visit her. When Nanda Kaul discovers that Raka, equally fond of solitude, avoids her company, she tries to win Raka's attention by relating a fantasy tale of adventure. Ultimately, Raka sets a fire in the forest around the house, an act symbolizing the burning away of Nanda Kaul's illusions.

THE VILLAGE BY THE SEA (1982). *The Village by the Sea* paints a picture of Indian rural life in a fishing village. Hari, who is twelve, and his older sister, Lila, live with a sick mother and an alcoholic father. Hari goes to Bombay to find a job and returns to his village; the story has a fairytale ending.

FASTING, FEASTING (1999). In *Fasting, Feasting,* Desai's third novel to be nominated for the Booker Prize, Desai returns to her theme of women's struggle for identity and independence in an Indian family. It also parallels two families, one in India and one in America, by juxtaposing their different attitudes toward food.

DIAMOND DUST: STORIES (2000). *Diamond Dust* is a collection of nine short stories; its characters cross cultural and geographical boundaries that span three continents, Asia, Europe, and North America.

Resources

There are no major collections of Anita Desai's manuscripts. However, students of Desai may be interested in the following Internet materials:

Anita Desai's Home Page is a valuable Web site for biographical and literary information about her (http://www.kirjasto.sci.fi/desai.htm).

Interview. One of Desai's most valuable interviews, in which she offers a fund of information about her childhood and her writing, is available on-line. Magda Costa, a book reviewer and e-publisher for RD Textos, interviewed Anita Desai in Barcelona on January 30, 2001 (http://www.umiacs.umd.edu/users/sawweb/sawnet/books/desai_interview.html).

Third World Views of the Holocaust. Desai here explains how she came to write the history of a German Jew in India in *Baumgartner's Bombay* (http://www.violence.neu.edu/Anita.Desai.html).

Voices from the Gaps. This page, which provides biography and criticism from the Women Writers of Color Web site, is another useful resource (http://voices.cla.umn.edu/authors/AnitaDesai.html).

HENA AHMAD

Index

Page numbers in **boldface** type indicate article titles. Page numbers in *italic* type indicate illustrations.